THE WAYS OF

PGA TOUR PLAYERS

Golf Tips from PGA Tour Players

TEAM GOLFWELL

The Ways of PGA Tour Players – Golf Tips from PGA Tour Players,

Copyright © 2021, Team Golfwell as to the collective work only. All rights reserved. No part of this book may be reproduced or transmitted in any form or by any means, electronic or mechanical, including photocopying, recording, or by any information storage and retrieval system, without written permission from the author, except for brief quotations as would be used in a review.

Contents

RORY MCILROY 1

"To avoid a hook, my takeaway thought is to make sure during those first three feet the clubhead works away wide and outside my hands, with a nice bit of loft on the club." 1

BRYSON DECHAMBEAU 9

"It was a quote from Hogan that I got early in my teens. He said, 'Every day that you're not working is another day somebody else is getting better than you.' And I took that to heart. Ever since then, I've always worked every single day as hard as I possibly can." 9

DUSTIN JOHNSON 16

"I can't play when I'm thinking about a bunch of technical things before I hit a shot. I'm not sure anyone can." 16

JORDAN SPIETH 26

"My caddie keeps reminding me, stay in the present, that is our mantra." 26

TIGER WOODS 34

"I can still see the shape of the shot in my mind when looking down at the ball." 34

JUSTIN THOMAS 41

"I like to experience a calmness when I play in a tournament and truly feel like I'm going to win the tournament." 41

RICKIE FOWLER 48

"I'm not your typical Tour Player. Feel and swinging free are important to me and I don't over worry about the outcome of the shot." 48

ADAM SCOTT 55

"I only use a single swing thought when I'm on the course." 55

JACK NICKLAUS 60

"I hit every shot in my mind twice, before I actually hit the shot." 60

JASON DAY 67

"My dad taught me never to give up." 67

PAULA CREAMER 72

"A good swing thought is to keep your height. Feel tall. Like your chest stays nice and high when you hit shots. This will help you maintain the width of your arms and prevent you from getting scoopy." 72

NICK FALDO 75

"I've faced many pressure situations and what you need is a great pre-shot routine" 75

KEEGAN BRADLEY 80

"I focus on my jaw muscles. When you can get your jaw to relax, this makes your whole body relax." 80

SERGIO GARCIA 86

"When I make practice swings on the tee I'm practicing for balance and tempo." 86

PHIL MICKLESON 90

"When I'm going for the pin, I stay aggressive, and I get more into the shot."
.... 90

ARNOLD PALMER 94

"Amateurs should putt from off the green if you can cleanly hit the ball, since their worst putt is usually better than their best chip." 94

JON RAHM 100

"If I don't believe in myself, nobody is going to do it for me." 100

BOBBY JONES 103

"You must be at ease, comfortable and relaxed at the address position." 103

BROOKS KOEPKA 107

"You have to stop yourself from thinking ahead. You can't start thinking about the trophy or about other things." 107

GREG NORMAN 112

"You have to be aggressive at this game." 112

Tried and True Advice 117

Creating Your Pre-Shot Routine and a Good Attitude 119

"Attitude will always win over ability... A golfer has to learn to enjoy the process of striving to improve. That process, not the end result, enriches life." – Dr. Bob Rotella, an excerpt from Golf is Not a Game of Perfect 119

Afterword 127

Thank You 129

About the Authors 130

The Ways of Golf's Greatests

Introduction

The perfect gift for the golfer in your life! Golf becomes easier knowing how the best in golf play and they'll love you for it. A great Father's Day gift, birthday gift, Holiday gift, or an ideal gift for any golfer.

From this treasury of exceptional quotes, advice, and information from PGA Tour players, the golfer will learn new pre-shot routines, swing thoughts, new aspects of the mental game, new techniques, and much more from top players like Phil Mickleson, Jack Nicklaus, Bryson DeChambeau, Brooks Koepka, Justin Thomas, and many others.

A golfer can decide what to put into their own game to improve their play and shoot lower scores. They don't have to search for it. It's all here in this book and having a reference book on what the greats do is extremely helpful to any golfer and great to keep on the nightstand.

The suggestions in this book also provide for great discussions on the 19th hole.

Even if this book only cuts 3-5 strokes off scores, it's well worth it!

RORY MCILROY

"To avoid a hook, my takeaway thought is to make sure during those first three feet the clubhead works away wide and outside my hands, with a nice bit of loft on the club."

Rory has recently improved his game with golf coach Pete Cowen who coached many PGA Tour players. Pete emphasized a balanced swing. "If you watch someone who hits it down the middle all the time, they swing within themselves, finish perfectly in balance and can hold that position for 20 seconds. Most golfers can't do that because their mechanics aren't good enough." Pete's coaching has helped Rory recently play better.

Rory has an interesting Cinderella-like background. He was born in 1989, stands 5'9" tall, and weighs 161 lbs. He's always credited his parents in helping him pursue golf. "My parents inspired and encouraged me to have a golf career," said Rory. "My dad coached me since I was small."

Rory's dad was a scratch golfer and his coaching certainly worked for Rory. "I saw my dad swing a club and I worked out how to do the same thing.

My backswing and follow-through have been basically the same since I was two years old."

His parents worked hard to give Rory, their only child the best opportunities in golf, as well as in life if the golf didn't work out.

Rory continued, "You know, I was an only child. My dad worked three jobs at one stage. My mom worked night shifts in a factory."

His father, Gerry said although it was tiring for his wife, Rosie, and himself, his wife would tell him, "Gerry, one day this could be all worthwhile."

How true. In 2011 at the age of 22, Rory was the youngest player to earn ten million euros in winnings. The next year, Rory was the youngest player to have won ten million dollars on the PGA Tour.

Rory visualizes, then aligns his shot in his pre-shot routine, and he emphasizes taking the club away in the first foot to two feet of his swing in one single piece. "I want everything — hands, arms, shoulders, club — all moving back together."

"I need to start back straighter, with the clubface looking at the ball longer, and let my body, hands, arms, shoulders, club, all move back together."

Rory said he uses only one swing thought. "I pick a spot about a foot in front of the ball and hit over it. That's the only thought in my mind. It takes my mind off the outcome of the shot and keeps me in the process."

Rory's thoughts when driving a ball on a hole he doesn't want to hook said, "To avoid a hook, my takeaway thought is to make sure during those first three feet, the clubhead works away wide and outside my hands, with a nice bit of loft on the club."

Rory has a positive attitude about pressure, "Obviously it has its stresses at some point, but at the same time it's where you want to be."

"We don't practice all these hours and grind away on the range and put so much work into it to be teeing off in the middle of the pack on Sunday of a major."

But Rory knows stress affects everyone. "The Masters is stressful. Is playing in the Masters stressful? Ask anyone who knows me, I'm a complete pr#ck the week before the Masters. But everyone knows that. It's very stressful. Pressure is self-inflicted and you put stress on yourself."

For swing thoughts, Rory said he sometimes uses the word "process" to help him put the shot in perspective which relaxes him, and "I don't try to make a huge deal about a shot -- it's just another golf shot."

"I think of the word 'process' to make a good choice, seeing the shot and make a good swing. That's all you can do."

If Rory has a must-make putt, he thinks of the word, "spot". Rory says, "I just roll it over a spot I picked about two or three inches in front of the spot. I don't think about whether I'll make it or not since I judge if I roll it over that spot, that's all I can do."

Rory added, "If the putt goes in, it's great, but if it doesn't, I'll try again the next hole."

Overall, Rory fights off pressure by thinking about making good contact. "If I have a tough shot or a moment where I really need to hit a good shot, I just think about making good contact, and that's all."

He explained, "It's simple. Take all out of your mind and make good contact and it all works out okay."

Rory is enthusiastic about fitness and goes to the gym regularly. "Going to the gym is great to keep in shape and be fit, and it's not only needed for your body, but it also helps clear your mind." He concentrates on balance and flexibility exercises. He stretches to increase his range of motion. He does cardio for his endurance, and numerous sets for strength endurance and overall strength.

One of Rory's goals is to increase his endurance, so he won't get tired on the golf course, and working on his balancing and stability to make him comfortable during a round of golf.

He does squats, jump squats, backward and side lunges with dumbbells, leg stretching, deadlifts, pull-ups, planks with leg raises for glutes, etc. Overall, he works his entire body.

Rory makes sure he eats right during a round. "On the course, I eat a little sandwich or an energy bar on the front nine and on the back nine."

"You're out there five hours, so you have to keep eating. You're going to burn at least 1,000 calories. I'll try to take in about 400-600 calories during a round and drink water."

This is what Rory eats if he's playing in the morning round, "If I'm playing in the morning, I'll get some carbs early like porridge with chopped banana."

If he's playing the afternoon round, "I'll start with less carbs and have some eggs and fruit for breakfast, then a light lunch about 90 minutes before I play, so I don't feel sluggish or full."

Maintaining an even emotional level has been difficult for Rory in past years, and he's been known to throw a club or two.

But Rory is, of course, aware of the importance of keeping a cool head. After a club throwing incident in 2015, Rory said, "Physically I feel fine, but mentally I could feel myself getting down on myself out there, which is not something I have been doing the last three weeks"

Rory says the way he handles the situation when he starts to get down on himself is simple, "I just need to make myself aware that I'm getting down on myself, and it's easier then to keep everything on an even keel."

Rory knows bad shots happen. "You have to just accept bad shots."

Rory uses swing thoughts to calm himself down and has been very successful in controlling his emotions. Rory says, when he's playing bad (like he did in the first round of the 2017 British Open), he doesn't get down on himself. "I had to find a couple of little key thoughts, and I feel like I have. I went with those on the second round, and it worked."

Rory said the gym workouts have helped him, "Going to the gym is great for your body, but it's also great for your mind."

Rory McIlroy has matured a lot and will become even more successful as he continues his golf career.

He is very thankful to his parents and said, "I want to make a point of basing myself at home, being close to my family. For what they did, they know they'll never have to work again, and I'll look after them."

He also wants to set a good example. "I realize I am a role model for a lot of kids who look up to me. I try to do my best in that regard and put myself across honestly and modestly."

Those words made many think of Rudyard Kipling's well-expressed thoughts about maturing when he wrote, "Meet with Triumph and Disaster and treat those two impostors just the same."

In any event, truly winning anything is done by just simply knowing you did the best you could with what you had at the time.

Rory said, "If you're not playing well, but you keep grinding away at it and still wind up winning, then you know you've accomplished something."

Having a good attitude and feeling comfortable is so important to winning. When Rory finally won at Quail Hollow in Charlotte in 2021, he said, "It felt like a long time since victory in China. The world is a different place than it used to be... "It just feels awesome. This is one of my favorite places in the world and to break the drought and win here again, it's awesome."

"It is never easy to win but it is a lot easier to win when you play well. The key is winning golf tournaments when you are not playing so well. Managing your game is something that I feel that I am still learning to do." - Rory McIlroy

BRYSON DECHAMBEAU

"The Scientist"

"It was a quote from Hogan that I got early in my teens. He said, 'Every day that you're not working is another day somebody else is getting better than you.' And I took that to heart. Ever since then, I've always worked every single day as hard as I possibly can."

Bryson is one of the most exciting players in golf currently. Especially when he drove and hit it 370 yards across the lake on the par 5 - 6th hole at Bay Hill. Here is a YouTube showing this>

https://www.youtube.com/watch?v=G2IDqiO3a7g

In 2019, Bryson decided to add mass to increase his swing speed and distance and added 20 pounds during the Covid pandemic and another 20 pounds during the suspension of play on the PGA Tour. He had a diet of carbs and proteins. "I've tried the keto diet and all these things, but what I've found is that as long as I'm keeping a 2:1 ratio of carbs to protein, that works for me."

After putting on more mass, he quickly led the PGA in driving distance. He explained, "Look, my body fat percentage has maybe gone up a percent or two, but it's not gone up that much at all. I would say a lot of it has been attributed to muscle. It's a lot of muscle."

When asked why he does the things he does, he simply replied, "That's what I've always been about is trying to shine a light on the game of golf and not push people away, with developing the one-length irons, having a new way of swinging the golf club and doing all these different things that look weird, but have been a massive benefit to the game, that's what I'm about." All his irons are 37.5 inches long (the usual length of a 7 iron). He uses the largest grips on the market as they help him better hold the club in the palms of his hands.

He also explained himself as a guy who tries to make things better. "I always look at the worst situations and try and figure out how I can make them better. Let today's garbage be better than yesterday's, is my motto."

He wants to be unique and himself and if you play by the rules of golf, there's nothing to prevent you to play your own unique style. "I feel like I've been able to bring an idea to the world stage and shine a light on a different way to play, an easier way. I want to change the game."

On why he decided to have clubs all the same length, he said, "You'll find that one-length irons are far more versatile around the greens. You can vary the trajectory more. Your distance control will improve because you can choke down more if you want."

Many people called the Wright Brothers lunatics for thinking they could have a machine fly. Bryson doesn't mind the critics, "Crazy is a relative term, you know. Everybody is unique in their own way and some people work harder for longer hours than others."

Bryson has said, "The search for information gives me more confidence because confidence arises from understanding."

He has maintained confidence, has a great attitude, and learns from his errors. "Most people are afraid of failure. I love failure because it tells me where to go next."

Bryson was born in Modesto, California in 1993 and lives in Dallas. He got a scholarship to SMU near Dallas, majored in physics, and was the first-ever SMU golfer to win the NCAA individual championship in 2015. He officially turned pro in 2016 and has won 8 PGA Tour events including one US Open.

Even though his nickname is "The scientist" he doesn't view himself as a brain, "I'm not really smart, but I'm dedicated. I can be good at anything if I love it and dedicate myself. And I love history. I love science. I love music. I love golf. I love learning. I love life."

Bryson has been criticized for slow play. He responded by saying, "The time to hurry is in between shots. It's not over the shot. It's timing how people walk. You must add that to the equation. If you've got somebody walking slow and they get up to the shot and take their 20 seconds, what's the aggregate time for them to hit that shot in between shots? That's what really matters. It's not the shot at hand."

He's also been criticized for taking too much time on his pre-shot routine. He argues, "People call me slow. I call myself quick with the stuff I do."

Before each shot, he checks 7 factors,

1. Air Density

2. Wind Vector

3. Elevation change

4. Local slope adjustment

5. The "roll out" number – and that is his estimate of where the ball will eventually stop.

6. Shape of the shot, and

7. He has a "secret factor" that he checks. Many thought his secret factor was dew point. But he doesn't want to reveal that but did say, "Dew point isn't the secret, but it affects the secret and I'm not going over that one. Intuitively the top players in the world know it, but they don't understand why it happens. I do."

Others may think this is not normal. But Bryson said he's not concerned with being normal. "I'm the one that's used to being not normal."

He accepts himself and makes his own way. "It's funny, I hear people say I'm faking all this science stuff. That's the furthest thing from the truth. It's literally what I have to do to play and perform at this level."

Bryson has a unique swing that he developed as his one of his goals is to have a perfectly repeatable swing. He has said playing golf is to find a solution to the game as you would find a solution to a puzzle.

As far as swing thoughts go, Bryson suggested you ask a coach to look at your swing and give you suggestions for what single thought you might want to have in your mind as you play a shot.

He reads putts in his own way. "I use a system called Vector Green Reading, which applies science to the green reads." This method considers the various slopes and Bryson uses a green book and occasionally a compass to help him map out the slopes.

Bryson uses the "arm lock" putting technique where the putter is locked to his leading forearm since he likes the "super smoothness" of it and high control. He uses this technique since, "Because I have something to brace it against and lock it in there, this allows me to be more repeatable."

His putting motion is stiff and robotic. He has said, "That allows me to repeat motion on a higher level. My arms are literally locked against my chest, and I raise my left shoulder up, and right arm goes down. I straighten the right arm. And I use the upper segment of my spine to move."

One very interesting record that Bryson shares with Jack Nicklaus and Tiger Woods is that he and Jack and Tiger are the only players ever to have won the US Amateur, NCAA Division 1 Champs, and three PGA Tour titles by the age of 25.

Like most of the PGA Tour pros, Bryson plays to win. "The only reason why I don't win is because of a bad decision, misjudged the wind, misjudged the read on the greens and wet conditions. Those are the three or four things that will cause me not to win. That's it."

He's also said, "That's my whole goal for the game of golf - it's not only to make myself a better player, but to have people have a more enjoyable experience when I'm around."

"People don't realize all the stuff I gave up growing up. I could have gone to parties and had fun at adventure parks with friends on weekends and things like that. But I went out and worked my butt off for eight hours playing golf."

DUSTIN JOHNSON

"I can't play when I'm thinking about a bunch of technical things before I hit a shot. I'm not sure anyone can."

Dustin doesn't say it's easy. "Anytime you're playing a major, the last four or five holes aren't going to be easy. There's never a guarantee. It's never easy."

Dustin Johnson is 6'4" tall, 190 lbs., and born in 1984 in Columbia, S.C. His father was a club pro, and Dustin began hitting balls when he was 6 years old. He also excelled in basketball and was a pitcher and a shortstop before he turned to golf at the age of 13.

Dustin qualified for the PGA Tour on his first try.

He fit in well with PGA Tour players easily, ranking in the top 5 during his first 6 years on tour.

While Dustin was growing up he always wanted to play pro golf. "I knew I would play golf and go to college."

He enjoyed watching the pro golfers and was amazed by John Daly's distance. "When I was a kid, I remember watching Daly bombing it at St.

Andrews in 1995 and winning the British Open. People say we are similar in a lot of ways."

Physical Training: Dustin does most of his resistance exercises balancing himself on one leg. For example, he does cable exercises standing on one leg, then does the same exercise switching to the other leg.

Dustin works on strengthening his upper body rotational velocity by throwing a 20-lb. medicine ball against a wall. He twists his upper torso as he holds the ball, takes a step forward, and throws the medicine ball as hard as he can against the wall 6 feet away to improve and maintain his rotational strength.

He works out daily. "I generally work out 2 hours each day," says Dustin, "and train my entire body over the week."

During the first 7 years he was on the Tour, he won at least one event every year. The only *other* golfer to win one event in 7 consecutive years was Tiger Woods.

Before playing a round of golf, Dustin warms up hitting wedges on the range, then he goes through hitting all his other clubs in order and finishes with his driver.

Dustin has the double E Factor: Emotional Equilibrium. He can control his emotions well. In 2010, Dustin took a 2-stroke penalty and eventually lost the 2010 PGA Championship at Whistling Straights for grounding his club in a waste bunker (the waste bunker was very subtle and didn't look like a hazard). He kept cool, shrugged it off, and took it in stride.

In the 2016 US Open, Dustin was given a late penalty for moving the ball with his putter on the 5th green during the final round. When this happened, Dustin stopped and asked an official about it since it was questionable whether his ball moved. The official at the 5th green didn't think it moved and told Dustin that.

Incredibly, after a telephone call from a TV viewer, other rule officials watched it again on TV. Those rule officials studied and studied it, then boldly decided there was a rule violation.

Then those officials reneged on what Dustin was told by the official at the 5th green and decided to tell Dustin (while he was just about to begin playing the 12th hole), that he was now penalized. Dustin controlled his emotions, kept his cool, and wound up winning by three strokes despite the annoying and unusual late penalty call.

Since then, the USGA rules officials decided they will not consider TV call-ins in the future to avoid this silly situation. The golf rules underwent major changes in 2019 including Rule 13 where the accidental movement of the ball on the green does not result in a penalty.

After being told he was going to receive a penalty, Dustin later said, "I just focused on my next shot and didn't worry about the penalty."

Barnard College President, and former University of Chicago Professor, Sian Beilock, Ph.D., is well-known for her research in the science of being emotionally upset and choking under pressure.

She researched golfers playing at the highest level. She found most problems occur in golf due to a player having too much time to mull things over between shots, where other sports require continued performance.

Dustin's method of keeping a cool head works very well since he doesn't mull over bad things. He has a high confidence level and loves challenges, knowing there isn't a shot in golf that others do, which he can't do himself.

"I don't get emotional when I'm playing well or bad. I try to stay on an even keel," Dustin said.

Another example of Dustin keeping himself in control occurred when he was playing the last three holes and the playoff holes at the 2017 Northern Trust Open at Glen Oaks. It was an exciting duel between Dustin and Jordan Spieth. Spieth was leading the tournament when the fourth round began. Dustin started the fourth round 5 shots behind him, and these two exceptional players wound up tied after finishing the fourth round.

During the last three holes of regulation play, each player made difficult shots and each of them sunk 20-foot putts under a great deal of pressure and wound up tied after 72 holes. Both Dustin and Jordan didn't take a lot of time analyzing their shots in the first playoff hole. Both handled the pressure very well.

On the second playoff hole, a 475-yard par 4 hole, Spieth hit a safe drive to the middle of the fairway which has water running down most of the left side of the hole.

Dustin drove next and decided not to take a safe route. He took a very risky shortcut over the water and hit a huge drive (341 yards) over much more of the water hazard, leaving only 95 yards to the pin.

Spieth was about 175 yards away and hit his second shot on the green, but the ball stopped about 30 feet away. Dustin then hit a wedge close to the pin and birdied to win the tournament.

When Dustin practices on the range, he begins his pre-shot routine making sure he visualizes and aligns the shot carefully. Dustin said he keeps a specific detailed picture of the shot in his mind, "How high, how much it curves, where it'll land, and where it will end up."

He then forces everything else out of his mind.

"I can't play when I'm thinking about a bunch of technical things before I hit a shot. I'm not sure anyone can."

He takes a good stance. He believes in having a good solid stance and that helps him make a good shot.

"By the time I'm in my stance, all I'm doing is picturing the shot and where I want it to go…."

He makes sure his knees are bent slightly, pushes his hips back (sits down), and puts his weights on his quadriceps.

Once he feels comfortable in his setup, he begins his takeaway making sure he maintains his correct setup during the first few feet of the takeaway. He said he uses a swing thought of staying in his stance which causes him not to sway, reach, or stand too tall over the ball. There are other times when he says he doesn't have any swing thought at all.

Once comfortable with his setup, he usually hits the ball quickly. He doesn't spend time letting other things enter his mind.

To summarize, Dustin goes into his pre-shot routine, then into his stance, and quickly executes the shot.

Dustin is also known as an excellent wedge player. He keeps a thought of keeping his left arm straight on the takeaway, so his upper left arm touches his chest at the height of his backswing.

"When I'm not playing well, it's usually due to having space between my straight left arm and my chest at the top of my swing. I want the inside of my left arm to be brushing or touching against my chest."

He goes through these thoughts on the practice range, but when he's playing, Dustin says, "I have one or two swing keys that I go with, but I'm not focusing on them in the few seconds before I play."

"I try not to get too emotional, whether it's going really well or going really bad, I always try to stay on an even keel -- which is great for golf, but it isn't always great for life.

His regular pre-shot routine keeps him from worrying about what's happened in the past, or what might happen. He doesn't think about much except for one or two swing keys like maintaining the correct stance during the first few feet of his takeaway. "There's nothing you can do about a bad shot. That's in the past so I forget about it."

Dustin is aggressive, "Telling me that I can't do something is probably the worst thing that anyone can say, because I'll definitely do it. I'm very determined."

On putting techniques, Dustin has said, "Golfers who try to make everything perfect before a putt rarely make it."

And "If I'm putting good, I win." Dustin switched to a longer putter in 2016 which allows him to keep his elbows slightly bent.

Right before going into the Northern Trust Tournament in 2017, he switched from his TaylorMade Spider Tour Black mallet putter and used a TaylorMade TP Collection Juno blade putter since he got a better feel with the Juno blade putter. "The longer shaft in the Juno blade allows me to hold it with my elbows bent giving me more feel with my hands."

Butch Harmon said Dustin has a fearless attitude and a lot of confidence in himself.

"Confidence levels go up and down on the PGA Tour," Butch said. Dustin used Butch as his coach in the past and is using Butch's son, Claude Harmon, III as his current coach.

John Rahm talked about Dustin after he played against him in the final round of the match play World Golf Championships. "I was amazed how Dustin kept cool the entire round…. He doesn't really make mistakes."

"I think he's learned from what he's done in the past and he's embracing it now and that's why he's winning tournaments."

Jon added a crucial point, "He doesn't ever get down on himself."

Not getting down on yourself, is the essence of Dustin Johnson. A very simple concept to incorporate into your game, and your life in general. Dustin simply does not mull things over criticizing himself.

In other words, he unconditionally likes everything about himself, the good things, the medium things, and the bad things.

We can be comfortable with who we are, no matter what if we smile and accept ourselves, despite what the pressures or problems might be.

Dustin respects his fans and fellow competitors and is a gentleman at all times since he knows the importance of fans and their support."

Dustin added, "I try hard to be a positive role model, especially on the golf course, and I try to respect everyone."

Dustin now has 24 PGA Tour wins including the 2020 Masters and received the Green Jacket from last year's amazing winner, Tiger Woods.

"When I'm on really tough golf courses, I feel like I'm more focused because I'm really trying to hit the ball to a certain spot, instead of, a lot of times, when I struggle sometimes is just staying mentally focused on every shot."

- Dustin Johnson

JORDAN SPIETH

"My caddie keeps reminding me, stay in the present, that is our mantra."

Jordan was born in 1993, 6'1" tall, and weighs 185 lbs. Jordan took an interest in golf at the age of 9. Jordan also played baseball, and his dad, Shawn Spieth, encouraged him and gave him a lot of support in playing baseball since Shawn played collegiate baseball.

But golf intrigued Jordan. "I felt golf was a game that you can never be perfect and that motivated me very much."

Jordan's father, Shawn seeing his son Jordan shoot a 62 at the age of 12, contacted Australian golf pro, Cameron McCormick, who was living in Texas at that time to arrange Jordan's first lesson. McCormick was later named PGA Coach of the year in 2015.

Jordan developed into a Junior Golf standout, then a star collegiate player for the University of Texas. He left halfway through his second year and joined the PGA tour at 19 years old.

Due to the heavy demands of traveling on the Tour, one of Jordan's highest priorities is to get at least 8 hours of sleep a day.

Jordan does gym work as well. His gym workouts concentrate on resistance training for strength in his muscles, flexibility, and endurance.

He does overhead deep squats, single-leg step-ups, planking, side planks, cable rowing, and emphasizes core body exercises.

He discusses all his golf shots and putting in detail with his excellent caddy, Michael Greller. Discussing shots does two things for Jordan:

1) Assistance in picking the right shot and visualization of the shot.

2) Jordan keeps in the present when discussing matters with his caddy about the shot. His mind is clear of past shots, as well as any past negative events.

Jordan doesn't think too much about the next shot until he is near the ball. He stays in touch with the present and doesn't reflect on much except the job at hand. He converses with his caddy about other things until they get near his next shot.

After Jordan won the British Open, he complimented Michael and said, "This is as much mine as it is his."

A weekend golfer usually doesn't have a caddy to talk to. But talk to yourself. Actor-comedian, Bill Murray agreed when Bill said, "Of course. I talk to myself. Sometimes I need an expert opinion."

Talking to yourself before taking a shot keeps you in the present. It's not awkward. Many golfers "Think aloud" while verbalizing and visualizing shots. Talking quietly to yourself is very helpful, especially after hitting a disastrous shot, and you want to put that shot out of your mind.

Jordan also takes his practice swings from behind the ball getting a feel of how he is going to hit the ball to his intended target.

He also discusses the shot with Michael as he takes a few swings. Jordan has said he thinks about and pictures in his mind similar shots he's made on the course, or the driving range.

Once Jordan has a feel for the shot, he addresses the ball by taking his stance. "I go to the basics. I check my setup, posture, alignment and make small adjustments from there," Jordan said.

Before he starts his swing, he looks up once more making sure he's aligned his body and feet correctly. If he feels uncomfortable about anything, he steps back and goes through his pre-shot routine again.

Jordan said he usually uses only one swing thought before he begins his swing. He tries not to cloud his mind with a lot of thoughts.

After the shot, he accepts the result and doesn't let the shot bother him too long if it was a bad shot. He believes when the shot is done, nothing can be done after that of course. He turns his thinking to the next shot forgetting about the past.

Swing thoughts mean having only one thought in your mind before hitting the ball, like "Make a smooth swing," or, "Make a full shoulder turn," for example.

Jordan has said he usually uses only one swing thought for an entire tournament. He then switches to a new swing thought at the next tournament. "I use only one swing thought instead of thinking about the tournament pressure," Jordan said.

The renowned golf coach, Jim McLean, said it's good to switch swing thoughts, "The mind is inherently inquisitive," said Jim. "The mind is always searching for freshness and old swing thoughts get stale."

Jordan had a disaster in the final round at the 12th hole at the 2016 Masters when he made 7 and eventually lost the tournament. How did he handle it? He didn't speak about it for a while. He put it out of his mind and continued playing.

Later, he didn't dwell on it ever again. He even joked about it during the 2017 Masters telling the spectators, "That shot was better than last year's," after he played the 12th hole again a year later in the first round.

Jordan's said his best putting is done when he's in "Blackout." He takes his time lining up a putt and then goes into "Blackout". He says he has no thoughts about his setup or stroke, or even the speed when he's in "Blackout". He allows his subconscious to take over.

He also suggested, "Look at the putt from behind the hole. Everyday players almost never do this. They should! Your eyes will take in more information about the slope. Sometimes you'll find that your initial read was incorrect."

"All I see is the arc of a putt with enhanced clarity like the gentle swoop of a 12-footer that breaks a foot. The ball's path alone is in my mind and nothing else."

Jordan explained it as, "My stroke is simply a reaction to make that path come alive and come to be with the roll of the ball."

For a time, he was missing very short putts three feet or less. To correct these yips, he began looking at the hole instead of placing his eyes over the ball when putting very short putts. That relaxed him and cured the yips.

Jordan feels very confident putting, "I focus on keeping the back of my left wrist flat and moving toward the target from start to finish. It's critical to do this."

One of Jordan's putting drills to help him control the speed of a putt is to take up an area on the green and begin the drill by placing a ball marker down about 5 feet away from the ball.

Jordan explained it as, "Putt to the marker, and stop the ball six inches past it or less."

"Then roll another putt trying to reach the first ball, but don't go more than six inches past it."

"If you can do that, then place the marker a bit further away, and so on, until the marker is about 10 feet away."

Jordan has talked about another putting drill he uses which trains him to hit a straight putt. "Find an area which is level for dead-straight putts of 10 feet on the practice green, and place two markers about 5 feet away from you. Space the two markers just far apart enough from each other to allow the ball to roll between them."

Jordan said, "I like to warm up doing this on the practice green. You must keep steady and make good strokes. It's perfect pre-round practice."

Jordan doesn't let the pressure of tour competition bother him. He reacts more as the pressure increases like when the going gets tough, the tough get going. "When the heat's on, I just focus more."

Jordan said weekend golfers shouldn't tense up. It isn't good to have tension in your hands when you address the putt or make the stroke.

"Tension turns your putting motion into a mess, especially on the putts 5 feet or less - the knee-knockers. Focus on the present and forget about missing it, and think positive, that will do it."

Jordan played a lot of golf with former President, George W. Bush. After Jordan won the British Open in 2017, he said, "I had two handwritten notes that were funny and extremely meaningful," Jordan said.

"One from President Bush... I played golf with him back in Dallas."

"President Bush jokingly said, 'I should give you some driving lessons.'"

"I've played with him, and I know I don't need driving lessons from him. Haha!"

Jordan was the world's number one ranked golfer on the World Golf Rankings for 26 weeks then didn't win a tournament since 201. He recently regained his momentum as a contender in PGA tournaments.

Spieth credits his comeback to making his swing shallower. He said, "It's kind of a change in the way the shaft's pitching so I can shallow it out, so I can clear out and get out in front of it. I had gotten steep for a while, which makes me back up and flip it, and I'm trying to get shallowed and cleared out to where I can get a more stable face and a lot more consistent ball-striking."

He came in 4th at the 2021 Waste Management tournament 2 shots down from the winning score. "I'm just trying to get out of the bad habits I got into … try to get back to what I did best that I didn't realize I did at the time," Spieth said at the Waste Management where he shot 61 in the 3rd round.

"My only focus after I start the putter away from the ball is keeping the back of my left wrist as fat as possible from start to finish. This is critical to keeping the putter head and ball moving straight down the target line after impact. It's also how Rory squares his putter face, and obviously it works for him."

- Jordan Spieth

The Ways of Golf's Greatests

TIGER WOODS

"I can still see the shape of the shot in my mind when looking down at the ball."

Tiger was born in 1975, stands 6'1" tall, and weighs 185 lbs. His father taught him how to play golf from the age of 2. Tiger said, "My Dad was my best friend, role model, coach, and mentor."

His father continued to coach him and by the age of 5, Tiger was winning tournaments against older kids. See this YouTube Video showing Tiger with Fran Tarkenton, when he was the ripe old age of 5. Tiger's swing then is very similar to the swing he has today.

https://www.youtube.com/watch?v=kfTY5xUFaJs

Although Tiger was blessed with a high degree of golfing ability, few people knew he worked very hard to get that way. "People don't understand that when I grew up, I wasn't the best, biggest, fastest or the strongest," Tiger said.

"The one thing I did was work at it, and that's why I succeeded."

"I've worked on the range for hours to compete at the highest level in major championships."

Tiger's practice sessions were lengthy when he competed in his teens. His practice sessions went up to 7-8 hours per day. "I hit various shots and practiced with all clubs. I shape shots, and I always try to keep range work interesting. After the range work, I practiced putting on the practice green."

After the practice green, Tiger spent his afternoon hours on the course working on his swing and practicing his short game.

Throughout his career, Tiger used the same pre-shot routine and didn't deviate from it. "I always try to stay in the same routine and same rhythm," Tiger said.

Tiger explained his pre-shot routine is what he likes, and other pros, of course, have different pre-shot routines. "They're all different," he said.

Tiger's pre-shot routine starts with the wind. If the wind is a factor, he will first toss blades of grass in the air to learn wind direction and force.

He takes a full view of the intended target, and trouble around the target such as bunkers, water, trees, etc. He discusses the yardage with his caddy and other points, e.g., bunkers or other hazards, etc.

If he's going for the pin, he'll get the exact yardages involved on everything around the green, e.g., yardages on bunkers, lakes, front of the green, back of the green, etc. Then he visualizes the shot and decides on the club he wants to use to get the ball there.

Steve Williams, Tiger's long-time caddy, wrote in his well-known book, "Out of the Rough," that when Tiger was pumped up and hitting the ball extremely well, he intentionally adjusted the yardage telling Tiger there was less yardage if Tiger started hitting the ball farther than normal.

Tiger routinely towels off the handle of the club he selects. Then, he takes slow practice swings while discussing the shot with his caddie and the yardages. He may throw more blades of grass now and then in the air when the wind is a factor.

He stands behind the ball and visualizes the shot he's decided upon. He pics a small target and aligns the shot.

He takes his stance and waggles the club, and then takes two to three full practice swings. After that, he'll take a waggle and begin to turn just his upper torso and shoulders, as a reminder to himself to turn his shoulders when he begins his swing.

He'll then take one more full practice swing before hitting the ball. Then, he looks at his target, looks at the ball, then looks at the target once more, then hits it.

If he feels uncomfortable during this pre-shot routine process, or if he just wants to look at the shot he's about to make again, he steps away and walks behind the ball, and goes through the identical pre-shot routine.

Tiger believes in having only one swing thought at a time, but when he putts, his only thought and vision is to see the ball going into the hole.

Tiger was known as one of the greatest putters in golf. He used the same pre-putt routine on every putt of some length. He is back competing in 2018 and still uses this pre-putt routine with a calm and somewhat less intense attitude when he was very young in lining up putts.

When he walks onto the green, Tiger takes in the contour, and the surroundings, then marks his ball. When it is his turn to putt, he replaces the ball and does a 9-step routine:

1. He walks halfway to the hole to see the second half of the putt and how it will break - if at all.

2. He then does a 360-degree walk around and views the putt from all perspectives. He stops occasionally to take in details, i.e., uphill, or downhill, left to right or right to left, etc.

3. During the 360-degree walk around, he stops at the hole, and looks down into the golf hole and studies the grain of the green by noticing the edges around the hole (smooth edges are with the grain and rough edges are against the grain).

4. After completing the walk around, he develops a feel on how the putt will break.

5. He then decides on the line, pace, and feel of the putt, and takes his stance. He takes two more practice strokes. He then looks up at the hole as he finishes the second practice stroke.

6. Then he places his putter behind the ball and aligns the putter head to where he wants it to start.

7. He adjusts his feet to get comfortable.

8. He takes one last look at the hole.

9. Then he hits the putt.

Tiger works out regularly when he is competing by working out five to six days per week. He stretches for 30 minutes, does high reps with weights (25 to 50 reps).

During the high number of reps, he focuses on his balance, control, endurance, and speed.

He changes his routine often varying the angle and exercises to cover all muscles. He works on strengthening the back muscles, and back shoulder muscles for good posture.

Tiger also eats a very strict and healthy diet when competing, focusing on eating lean meats, seafood, lots of fruits and vegetables and, avoiding junk food.

For breakfast, he eats an egg-white omelet with vegetables. Lunch and dinner were mostly grilled chicken or grilled fish with salad and vegetables.

Tiger is working his way back on tour in 2018 and he is a competitor. Long ago, he said during an interview in 2006 on CBS TV, "I love to compete. That's the essence of who I am." If he can compete at the level he competed at in the past, his efforts should bring a lot of excitement.

All of that became true at the 2019 Masters that he won showing one of the greatest sports comebacks in history. He is recovering from a serious car crash in California. Millions of fans expressed get well wishes to him on social media.

"There's no sense in going to a tournament if you don't believe that you can win it. And that is the belief I have always had. And that is not going to change."

-Tiger Woods

JUSTIN THOMAS

"I like to experience a calmness when I play in a tournament and truly feel like I'm going to win the tournament."

Justin Thomas was born in 1993 and is 5 feet 10 inches tall and weighs 155 lbs. Justin naturally wanted to be a golf pro as his dad and granddad were pros and Justin began swinging a golf club at the age of 2.

Justin was also inspired to play professional golf after he watched Tiger Woods win the 2000 PGA Championship at Valhalla Golf Club in Louisville when he was 7 years old.

Justin was brought up well being taught to keep a positive attitude when the difficulties of the game surfaced. He said, "My parents treated me the same whether I shot 66 or 76."

Justin said the best advice his father ever gave him was to enjoy life. Even though Justin's father and grandfather were both golf pros, Justin wasn't in any way forced to follow suit. He was only told no matter what he decided to do in life, he should "just enjoy it."

Justin competed in Junior Golf and met Jordan Spieth at an All-Star Junior Golf Tournament. This was the first time he competed against Jordan. They both shot 68 on the first round of the two-round event. Spieth went on to win the second round. Later they became good friends are still very good friends today.

Justin didn't have immediate success on PGA Tour compared to the overnight success Jordan Spieth experienced.

But Justin's day was coming. He began to do very well on tour in 2016, winning the CIMB Classic in October, then went on to win two more tournaments in January 2017.

He was exceptional at driving the ball, and at putting using a Scotty Cameron specially made and adjusted X5 putter.

Justin always wanted to improve at putting and had a great streak in putting well which began in late 2016. This was a result of Justin meeting with Scotty Cameron about the putter he made for Justin and asked Scotty to study his putting stroke in the workshop. Scotty watched Justin putt, then to correct Justin's tendency to hit it slightly right of the target, Scotty adjusted the lineup line upwards just a minute amount on the putter head, and it made all the difference.

2017 proved to be a momentous year for Justin when he won the PGA Championship and the FedEx Cup Championship. He won Player of the Year on the PGA Tour.

He said his 2017 success arose gradually as he learned how to become more patient with his game. To fight off impatience, Justin gradually let things happen and didn't rush his game.

Justin averages over 300 yards driving the golf ball. Pound for pound, he's one of the longest hitters.

Studies have been done on Justin and his ball-striking ability. Dr. Robert Neal, a well-known golf physicist, found Justin has an extremely high percentage of strikes exactly in the center of the face of his driver more than most players.

Justin excels at hand and eye coordination. His swing speed is almost 120 mph and adding that speed to his unusual ability to hit the ball on the sweet spot makes him an exceptional driver of the golf ball.

He handles pressure well. When most golfers experience a lot of new success, the golfer tends to put pressure on himself to keep winning. Former PGA Star, Hal Sutton, went into a slump after winning several tournaments, then Hal began putting too many expectations on himself.

Although Justin is sometimes emotional, he doesn't let the pressure get to him. His father knows Justin can be fiery, but remarked Justin showed a lot of maturity and patience when he won the PGA Championship in 2017. "He's very fiery. He's very emotional and he's very aggressive," his father, Mike Thomas said, "But, he showed a lot of patience and maturity winning the PGA."

Justin said during the PGA Championship, he had a quietness about himself. "I was calm all week and felt like I truly would win."

To maintain his flexibility, Justin stretches each day for at least 15 minutes. "I focus on flexibility, width, rotation, balance and swing plane," Justin said, and he learned this from his father.

He works out as he travels on the PGA Tour but doesn't use a lot of weights in his workouts. He does deep squats to maintain his legs and glutes with a resistance band. He uses the resistance band for overhead presses to strengthen the small muscles around his shoulder blades, and for stability in his upper shoulders.

He also uses the resistance band doing monster walks, which strengthen the muscles around his knees and glutes. He does "Discus turns" which are done by transferring his weight from right to left by turning as quickly as he can as if throwing an imaginary discus.

He does one-legged squat jumps for balance control, and to strengthen his quadriceps. He does cable twists transferring his weight from his right side to his left side to exercise his obliques and does other exercises centered on strengthening his core muscles.

Justin tries not to think about the next shot until he gets near his ball. While walking, he tries to stay as natural as can be and takes in the surroundings as he approaches the ball.

Justin has a simple pre-shot routine that keeps negative thoughts out. He begins by standing behind the ball and visualizes where the ball is going to go and how he wants to hit it there. He aligns his shot on the path he wants for the ball to follow, then takes his stance.

He settles into his stance adjusting his feet for the correct ball position for the shot he wants to play. He looks up at his target once more, then looks down at the ball again.

If he doesn't feel at ease, he continues looking up at his target until he feels more comfortable, especially with his alignment.

Once he is ready, he takes a slight pause, then hits the shot.

As he hits his shot, his head remains still, and he doesn't look up to see the shot until his right shoulder passes under his chin raising his head.

It's almost as if his head is unable to raise up by itself unless it is brought up by his right shoulder and upper torso.

Justin doesn't take much time for a pre-shot routine. PGA Tour players average about 30 seconds to do a pre-shot routine. Some take less time and others take more. Kevin Na sometimes takes over a minute or more. Kevin has been successful on tour and he is an example top player that doesn't have to have the same pre-shot routine before each shot.

Justin usually uses one or two swing thoughts, "I think everybody has at least one or two swing thoughts. Mine change from week to week, month to month, or day to day - if I'm not playing well."

Justin has one thought when he begins his golf swing. "I usually think about the yardage and the shot, in general, that I'm trying to hit."

Justin started his pro career on the Web.com Tour. "I think the biggest difference between being out on the PGA Tour and the Web.com Tour, is being able to chip it to within two feet (which you need to have on the PGA Tour) and chipping it to five or six feet on the Web.com Tour. You're going to make a two-footer, but you'll miss one or two 6-footers."

The essence of Justin Thomas is he's becoming more patient on tour, and it's made all the difference with him. Justin is very used to winning having won numerous tournaments before earning his PGA Tour card through the Web.com Tour.

His well-known and experienced caddy, Jimmy Johnson (who caddied for Nick Price and Steve Stricker), said "He's been steadily improving, and the more patient he is, the better he plays."

Justin continues to win on Tour. He's won the 2018 Honda Classic in a playoff over Luke List. The 2019 WGC-Bridgestone Invitational by 4 strokes over Kyle Stanley. The 2019 BMW Championship by 3 strokes over Patrick Cantlay, the 2019 CJ Cup at Nine Bridges by 2 strokes over Danny Lee, and the 2020 Sentry Tournament of Champions in a playoff over Patrick Reed. He's won the 2020 WGC-FedEx St. Jude Invitational by 3 strokes and the 2021 Players Championship recently won the 2021 Tournament Players Championship by one shot over Lee Westwood.

"My attitude is good because I'm a fierce competitor and I have all the confidence in the world that I can beat everybody else. That's my attitude.

-Justin Thomas

RICKIE FOWLER

"I'm not your typical Tour Player. Feel and swinging free are important to me and I don't over worry about the outcome of the shot."

Rickie is 5' 9" tall and weighs 150 lbs. and was born in 1988. His grandfather started taking him to the range when Rickie was 2 where he loved to hit balls and putt on the practice green.

Rickie said, "My grandpa took me to the range when I was about two and showed me how to hit a ball and I grew up playing."

Rickie also loved to race motocross but gave it up at 15 devoting most of his time to golf competitions.

Rickie has been financially successful from his golf career, but he didn't come from a wealthy background. "I didn't come from money. My parents both worked really hard to keep food on the table and give my sister and I opportunities to play sports."

Rickie Fowler thinks about other things between shots. "I play my best when I keep the technique simple."

Rickie likes to keep things simple and knows too much thinking about the different facets of a golf shot is not a good way to play golf.

"I'm one to truly swing free and not worry about the result. You have to trust your swing and let it go."

Barry McDonnell, a cigar-smoking local golf pro, taught Rickie the golf swing. "We started working together when I was 7," said Rickie. "But he'd smoke his cigar while I hit away."

Rickie said, "We never laid sticks on the ground for alignment, and we never used a video camera - I don't think he knew how to operate one."

Rickie said Barry taught him how to align the clubface and work on ball flight, "and making sure the ball was starting where I wanted it to." Barry showed Rickie how to change the flight of the ball, i.e., higher, or lower, draw or fade, which made shot-making very interesting to Rickie vs. just hitting one ball after another.

And Rickie loved the game. "I spent years on the range while I was growing up," said Rickie.

Before he went to Butch Harmon, Rickie played a long time without a personal coach.

That was because he was playing well and if it's not broke, why fix it? "I play my best when I keep a clear mind and keep my swing simple."

Rickie, as most every golfer, doesn't like slow play. He said you can't score well when there's slow play since you tend to overthink shots and too much thinking isn't good to keep your brain fresh.

Rickie recommends not to get yourself mentally fatigued in a slow play situation. "When there's slow play, talk with your playing partners about anything and think about each shot for a minute and not much more than that. You'll stay fresh."

"I used to consider yardage, take in hazards, and overthink shots. My caddie told me I play better when you only think about the distance you want to fly the ball."

"I see golfers who are too quick with their backswing," said Rickie. And Rickie says he does that as well, "One of my tendencies is to be too quick on the downswing and the club gets behind me and the ball could go anywhere."

"When I need a drive on the fairway going into the final holes, I think only about making a slow and deliberate backswing, and not to be too quick at the top."

"Beginning with a slow and deliberate backswing, makes it much easier to make a smooth transition."

In Rickie's pre-shot routine, he takes his stance then waggles the club making sure he feels comfortable before he takes the shot and makes any adjustments to make himself comfortable. When his coach was Butch Harmon, Butch suggested for Rickie in his pre-shot routine to take the club halfway back, then return it to his stance before hitting the ball.

Rickie said this helps him to stop himself from getting his shoulder to dip or turn to lower his torso as he takes the club back. This gives him more consistency with his swing and the resulting shot.

Rickie attends weekly Bible study while he's on tour and is serious about his spirituality.

Rickie routinely does gym work. He had a problem putting pressure on his lower spine due to over-rotating his hips.

Rickie was told having strong legs and glutes will help tone down overactive hips. So, he had his trainer give him routines to strengthen his lower body which stops over-rotating his hips and prevents back pain.

Rickie worked on legs and glutes by doing side squats with dumbbells working one leg at a time. He concentrates on glute and leg exercises to get more control turning and opening his hips.

The nature of Rickie Fowler is he is confident with his golf ability and knows he can play very well. He doesn't overthink his shots. "I like to swing and let it fly," said Rickie which is due to him spending many hours at the range when he was a small boy, and just letting his natural ability take over.

Rickie's last win on the PGA Tour was the 2019 Waste Management Phoenix Open by two shots over South Africa's Branden Grace. With 5 PGA Tour wins, many expected him to win more when he joined the Tour after being the star player at Oklahoma State.

Like Jordan Spieth who went through a slump, Rickie appears on the way out of his slump by finishing in the top 10 in the 2021 PGA Championship 5 shots out of the lead on an extremely difficult golf course.

Slumps are tough as he's recently said, "It's tough for all of us that are involved, from my caddie to my wife having to deal with me at home. I'm trying to be the best husband that I can, not bringing golf back home. But when you're out on the road that long and on the grind, putting in the work at home -- it's pretty much been all golf."

He explains trusting yourself is important. "I'm not your typical Tour Player. For me, golf is about feel and swinging free, like you couldn't care less about your results. I know that might be hard to accept, especially if you've been struggling to hit the ball straight or have contact issues but hear me out. When you're able to build trust in what you're doing and simply "let it go," power creeps into your swing as if by magic."

US Open Champion Graeme McDowell is of the same thinking, "You turn off your mind. You feel your golf swing without really thinking about it. It's almost like you don't think at all. Maybe you have one little thought, and everything else becomes automatic."

Rickie has said during his slump he was asked, "'Have you been able to fish much at home?' Not really. It's been workout, therapy, and golf...But we're all in this together, and we're going to keep battling it out. It's been frustrating. I'm ready to be past that."

He remains positive and has many fans supporting him.

"I've had a great run so far out here... But at the end of the day, we get to play an amazing game for a living ... we have it pretty darn good out here, and we have fun."

ADAM SCOTT

"I only use a single swing thought when I'm on the course."

"Whatever I'm working on, I like to keep one swing thought in my head when I'm on the course. Keeping it simple helped me at the Deutsche Bank Championship in Boston last year. Thinking only about getting to my left side, I shot 62 Friday and won my first PGA Tour event."

Adam was born in 1980, and stands 6 feet tall, and weighs 180 lbs. He began playing golf when he was 4 and was coached by his father, a PGA club pro.

His father taught him only the fundamentals of golf as he didn't want to give Adam too much information on detailed technical things at an early age. His father has said, I didn't want to crowd his mind with too many technical thoughts."

Adam eventually beat his pro father at golf when he was 13 years old.

Adam played for the UNLV golf team and then turned pro. He began on the European Tour where he won ten times.

"Winning a major championship is what most golfers want to do."

Adam said his caddie, Steve Williams, talked with him before playing the first hole in the first round at the 2012 British Open, "We discussed mindset since I usually play well when the majors take place, but I generally wasn't playing well in the first round."

"Steve suggested I go to the first tee of the first round and play it like it was the 72nd hole which I need to birdie, and that helped my attitude."

But Adam eventually lost the tournament in the final round. He led by four shots with four holes to play, "Next time, I'm sure there will be a next time, I'll do a better job," said Adam briefly discounting the disappointing finish – and not dwelling on it.

Most people would have great difficulty after a heartbreak loss at the Open like Adam went through. He knew he was a great golfer and one "Mess up" doesn't mean, "Give up" in Adam's attitude.

The best part about losing is that it's only temporary, as Adam came back strong and won the Masters the following year in a dramatic pressure-filled playoff sinking a difficult 12-foot putt with the help of an excellent read by his caddie, Steve Williams.

Greg Norman inspired Adam. Adam said, "Greg Norman is an icon in Australia, not only because he was the best player in the world, but because of the way he handled himself with so much grace through the years. He was my role model."

When Adam won the 2013 Masters, he said, "Part of this is for Greg. I drew on him today. He's given me a lot of time and he's given me inspiration and belief through the years, as well as inspiring all of Australia."

Adam doesn't cloud his mind before a shot. He believes in only have one swing thought when he's playing a round of golf.

"Keeping it simple helped me at the Deutsche Bank Championship in Boston last year."

"My swing thought was thinking only about getting to my left side. Using that, I shot 62 Friday and won my first PGA Tour event."

Adam focuses on the fundamentals of his pre-shot routine. He first visualizes the shot traveling to his target and then aligns the shot. Then checks his grip (he uses a neutral grip generally) to make sure he can see two and a half knuckles on his left hand.

He takes his stance and with a standing tall posture as well as making sure he is playing the ball in the correct position between his feet.

Adam, in his late 30s, is physically fit. He keeps working out to maintain fitness and his flexibility by stretching exercises including balancing exercises.

The Golf Channel featured Adam and his trainer showing what Adam does to maintain himself and begins with a hip flexor stretch. http://www.golfchannel.com/video/titleist-performance-institute-stretching-adam-scott/

The essence of Adam Scott is that he enjoys his life and takes pleasure in playing golf. He likes his job. "You know, I go to work in a great office every day, and the amount of freedom that goes with being a pro golfer on the tour is awesome."

"So, I get to enjoy my weeks off away from the course, and then I get to go to work on some of the best golf courses in the world out here."

Adam has 14 wins on the PGA Tour and his last win was the 2020 Genesis Invitational by 2 strokes over runners-up, Scott Brown, South Korea's Kang Sung-hoon, and Matt Kuchar.

Adam has a saying he uses to keep his spirits up and stay positive as he continues to compete again much younger players.

"If all else fails, birdie the last."

    - Adam Scott

JACK NICKLAUS

"I hit every shot in my mind twice, before I actually hit the shot."

Jack was born in 1940 and stands 5' 10" and was born in Columbus, Ohio. His father, Charlie was a scratch golfer and an excellent tennis player.

Jack also played tennis, football, baseball, and other sports, and played his first 9 holes of golf when he was 10 years old and shot a 51.

Some debate exists on who is the greatest golfer of all time. Some say due to Jack's consistency and his ability to win more major tournaments requiring the high golfing skills on the toughest and most difficult courses that Jack was certainly one of the greatest.

As we all know, major tournaments require brilliant golf minds, endurance, experience, and many other requirements most of us don't possess. Moreover, the golf courses on which major tournaments are played have extremely narrow fairways and deep and difficult rough.

Jack won 18 major titles and came in second 19 times (discrediting the adage, "No one remembers who came in second") on very difficult demanding courses with the toughest competition.

Another side of the debate on who was the GOAT rests on an argument of which golfer dominated his competitors to a very high degree and argue Tiger far exceeded the second place scores off his competitors, making Tiger was one of the greatest golfers.

It's still a matter of long debate. Frankly, most believe Jack and Tiger don't want to debate GOAT issue. It doesn't seem to matter to either one of them who is considered the best golfer of all time, although Tiger is known for his desire to break every golf record on the books especially the most wins at major tournaments.

Both feel they did the best they could with what they had in their golf career, and that in and of itself is winning, and being the greatest you can be is a true personal victory. Any golfer who can honestly say to themselves they played their best is already a winner. What do you as the reader think?

Jack's pre-shot routine is simple and remained the same during his entire playing career. He would stand behind the ball and survey his surroundings taking in all the factors important to him, then he would focus on a specific target and visualize how to hit the ball there.

He recommends swinging smoothly when you need to make an important shot. "I've always thought the phrase "hit it nice and easy," when a golfer needed a big shot, was dopey advice. 'Hit it nice and smoothly' sounds much better to me."

On swing thoughts, Jack suggested, "The time to focus your mind on key swing thoughts is when you settle into your final address position."

Jack was excellent in course management. "You need to manage every shot and discipline yourself and play shots for position," Jack remarked.

"Precision in playing is more important than hitting a long ball," Jack said.

Even if Jack was hitting it badly, his course management skills made him win, "A big part of managing a golf course is managing your swing on the course. Its surprising many players have no idea how to play for position and how to manage the ball and the shot. I've won even though I was hitting the ball badly."

Hale Irwin said, "Jack thought his way around the golf course better than anyone else."

Going back to Jack's pre-shot routine, Jack would discuss the yardage with his longtime caddy, Angelo Argea, and visualize the shot and select a club to hit it to his target.

Jack was extremely consistent. He kept his pre-shot routine, swing, etc. the same over the years. He shaped his well-thought-out shots with precision.

Jack had a method of aligning his shot. He would select a specific target, then draw a line back from his target to his ball selecting a blade of grass or spot about 3 to 4 feet in front of his ball in direct line with his target.

He would take his stance and his left foot would be turned slightly outward. He would take one or two waggles with his club as a reminder to stay loose.

When he was ready to hit the ball, he triggered each swing by first turning his chin about an inch or two to the right before turning his shoulders, arms, and club to begin the swing.

When asked how he handled pressure during play, Jack said he avoided pressure ruining his game by focusing. "Focusing on shots blocks out pressure."

And Jack wasn't one to look for excuses as he feels that will make you lose your concentration and when that happens you start to feel the pressure again.

Frank Beard, one of Jack's competitors said, "The mental side? Nicklaus was the best. He was organized, maintained his discipline and composure. I never saw him lose his cool."

Gary Koch said, "Jack was always on an even keel. That allowed his mind to work at its best. Jack had great emotional stability."

Jack said, "You've got to have confidence which comes from working hard at golf, or at anything you do in life.?

He also knew the importance of the mental game as well before that subject became widespread. He explained he felt it was important "to have confidence in your mind so you can hit the shot you want to hit and not wonder about when the next bad shot is going to happen."

When it came to putting, Jack admitted he didn't have a pre-putting routine. "I don't have a set routine which might force me to putt before I felt comfortable."

He took his time on the green until he felt comfortable. When asked about this he simply said, "Getting comfortable worked for me."

Jack also needed to get a "feel" for the putt before he'd hit it. "I keep my grip pressure light and constant. I controlled the putter more with my right hand and with my right arm."

Jack had a well-known crouch (almost hunchbacked) when he putted so he could visualize the line of a putt. He said he did this since he was left-eye dominant. And, crouching over the putt with an open stance, making it easier for him to see the putting line with his left eye.

Jack also said, "I hold my breath during and just prior to making the putting stroke. Preventing the diaphragm from moving helps me to keep my body and head perfectly still."

The crowd at Augusta was going wild in the 1986 Masters with Jack sinking amazing putts with the oversized zero-twist Response putter as well as his amazing shots shooting 65 on the final day.

The roars of the crowd as Jack made putts also put other players off their game.

Jack was a long hitter with a lot of power. He was the first major player to have that ability. He remarked, "Today, they all seem to play with power."

To summarize the play of Jack, Johnny Miller perhaps put it best, "Jack's not a normal competitor. He's the only guy I know who is pleased to see someone make birdies. That makes him more competitive, and he plays better. He's very disciplined."

Jack viewed competitive golf brilliantly by just wanting to beat the course and wasn't concerned with other players or trying to beat a certain player. He just loved to play the course and see how well he could manage his play which most agreed he did exceptionally well.

"Pursue what you love…. Don't let anyone else tell you what your life path should be."

- Jack Nicklaus

JASON DAY

"My dad taught me never to give up."

Jason Day was born in 1987 and stands 6 feet tall and weighs 195 lbs. David Feherty asked Jason how he learned to golf, and Jason explained it wasn't easy for him.

Jason, whose father died when Jason was a young boy, went to a school having a golf program where Jason met coach, Colin Swatton (who later caddied for Jason on tour).

Colin said, "When I taught Jason how to play golf and showed him how to do something, say one of the fundamentals of golf, Jason would do it repeatedly until he could do it. And that quality was something none of the other students had."

Colin explained, "The other students would get bored with a fundamental and move on, but Jason kept at it until he had it completely mastered."

Tiger Woods' book "How I Play Golf" (he borrowed it) also influenced Jason, and Jason was determined to match Tiger's scores. "I practiced in the early morning, at lunch, and in the evening continually."

Jason got to know Tiger and they have a good relationship to this day.

Jason previously used a unique pre-shot routine that began with standing behind the ball, then visualizing the shot he wants to make, and briefly looks at aligning the shot.

He then shuts his eyes to envision himself swinging and making the shot. He creates a movie of himself in his mind taking his stance, then making the kind of swing with the exact tempo he wants to make to hit the shot.

Keeping his eyes closed, he envisions the ball flying on the arc in the way he wants it to fly to his intended target. He practices deep breathing while he does this behind the ball getting more oxygen into his lungs and to his brain making him more relaxed.

When he opens his eyes, he aligns the shot and then and slowly and comfortably takes his stance.

He flexes his knees and goes into a relaxed stance and adjusts his footing a few times.

He grips and regrips the club with hand pressure about 5 on a scale of 1-10.

He takes one or two waggles lifting the club up and down behind the ball. Then he brings the club back behind the ball reminding himself to do a wide takeaway if he's hitting off the tee. And right after he's done with the short wide takeaway reminder, he simply does a nice smooth swing.

Jason said he creates more power driving the ball this way, "As I start my backswing, I know the wider the arc, the more power I can generate." said Jason. I visualize the clubhead on the outside rail of a set of railroad tracks and my hands above the inside rail. This creates a wide swing arc. The wider the arc, the more power I can generate."

Jason does this is to keep himself in the present not allowing any other thoughts to enter his mind. He completely devotes his present attention to making the shot in a routine and comfortable way.

Jason's visualization methods are a great way to stop repetitive bad shots. Slowing down and visualizing should get you back to your usual game.

Jason works out in the gym with exercise programs like the programs of Dustin Johnson.

He had worked out before but didn't work his legs enough. "My upper body was too big. It's difficult to play golf with a large upper torso and a small lower one," Jason said.

So, he emphasized working his legs more. "You've got to have big strong legs and a strong core. So, I do a lot of squats, do a lot of trap-bar deadlifts, and a lot of sumo deadlifts."

Jason also cut out eating carbs to lose weight and become more fit. Then he found himself getting tired on the course. "I had to start eating a lot more carbs. I take in about 800 to 1,000 calories during a round, two or three protein bars and a protein shake, so that I'm constantly eating. I keep hydrated as well on the golf course."

The essence of Jason Day, a former #1 world-ranked golfer, is a discipline with a never-give-up attitude. He has said, "You could have all the tools in the world, but if you really don't want to be there, or if there's something that's off course that's playing on your mind... the game of golf is so mental, and if you don't have everything in the right order, it's very difficult to win golf tournaments."

He last won in 2018 winning the Farmers Insurance Open in a playoff over Alex Noren and

Ryan Palmer. He also won the 2018 Wells Fargo Championship by two shots over Nick Watney and Aaron Wise.

Jason has been in a slump although the great years he previously had can't ever be taken away. But he keeps positive and patient.

"I'm getting better and better each year that I'm playing golf on the world stage, and finishing runner-up only teaches you how to continue being patient - something that is key to our game."

- Jason Day

PAULA CREAMER

"A good swing thought is to keep your height. Feel tall. Like your chest stays nice and high when you hit shots. This will help you maintain the width of your arms and prevent you from getting scoopy."

"Standing Tall" is highly recommended among many teaching pros. Stand in the same position as a linebacker in football. Head up, torso long, butt out. This linebacker position allows you to rotate easier rather than feel like you must reach down to hit the ball. Tiger, Adam Scott, Sergio all do this well.

Paula won the US Women's Open in 2010 among her 12 professional wins in her career. She started playing golf at the age of 10 and then won 13 consecutive junior events in Northern California and was ranked at #1 in California.

As she succeeded on the LPGA tour, she shared her desire for success that came from simply her love of the game, "I love to win. But probably equal to that - I love doing what I do."

Golf is fun and it is also a way to better business. Paula shared her experiences in playing in pro-ams where she learned golf was a vehicle for success in business for women. "Women in pro-ams are always telling me about all the business deals they've struck on the golf course playing with their male work colleagues."

Her advice to golfers who want to get better is "Find a good teacher that will keep the game fun. Work hard and don't be afraid to have success or disappointment. That is what golf is all about."

Her advice for her scoring better and to other golfers is to "Practice, work out, proper nutrition, lots of work on the short game. In golf, that's really where the strokes come off the scorecard."

She has said her best swing thought is to imagine herself swinging while she is standing in a barrel. She thinks that to prevent herself from swaying back and forth as she tends to sway. "I tend to sway and not load and use my lower half."

She thinks of standing in a barrel so she can load up on her right side and turn and shift to her left side and end the follow-through with her weight on her left heel.

Also, when she does her pre-shot practice swing, she swings with her right foot placed behind making it easier for her to do a full turn and that also reminds her to make a good turn.

She also had a slight pause at the top of her swing because she tends to be too quick on the downswing and slowing down at the top gives her better timing and more distance to her shots.

"As an American champion, obviously being here in the states, is something that we all look at with the U.S. Open. But golf is played all over the world, and there are so many great golfers from other countries, and we're lucky enough that this is our home base to be able to play out of."

- Paula Creamer

NICK FALDO

"I've faced many pressure situations and what you need is a great pre-shot routine"

Sir Nick Faldo, born in 1957, stands 6' 3" tall and weighs 195 lbs. He began golfing at the age of 14 and was inspired to play after watching Jack Nicklaus win the 1971 Masters.

Nick won 41 professional golf tournaments, including 6 major tournaments (he won the Masters 3 times and the Open 3 times) and was ranked #1 in the world. Nick simply said he loved the fascinating game of golf and it just simply agreed with him. Nick has become a very successful TV golf analyst.

Nick suggests not to overthink the game. "Sit, coil, pull, release. Simplicity is the answer to a great golf swing."

Nick mentions he was taught a practice routine to try and hit an iron softly at first (say hit a 7 iron 100 yards, with 50% power), then to gradually increase his swing up to 80% power. Nick suggests not to try to hit the ball with more than 80% of your power.

For pre-shot routines, he recommends once you've determined the distance and selected your club, the next step is visualization, then alignment, "It's obvious that it is no good having a perfect setup, perfect grip and perfect golf swing if the whole thing is misaligned."

"It sounds obvious, but many players simply do not spend enough time getting themselves on target."

Nick also believes the most important part of his pre-shot routine is the practice swing.

Nick refers to the practice swing as a "Rehearsal" of exactly what you are going to try to do with the shot. He recommends before taking your stance, simulates what you are about to do.

"Don't just look at your target and say to yourself, 'Oh, I just want to hit it about 100 yards,' then go into your stance without a practice swing and hit the ball," says Nick.

Nick does practice swings behind the ball, or next to the ball - wherever he finds it most comfortable. Then he rehearses hitting the shot. "Hit an imaginary ball to your target practicing your swing at the exact tempo you intend to use."

When you do this rehearsal, don't let anything else enter your mind. "Block anything else completely out of your mind other than what you exactly want to accomplish with this shot."

Then, Nick says, if you feel comfortable, "Step straight in, and hit the shot."

Nick believes if you are blocking everything else out other than what you are about to do with the shot, and you've rehearsed the shot hitting an imaginary ball, "Your mind adjusts easier from the rehearsal and the real thing."

Tempo is important to Nick, "Tempo is the glue that sticks all elements of the golf swing together."

Nick is fit and says watching what you eat and how much you eat is vitally important. "If you want to play better, you must eat better, you have to look out for yourself."

Nick has a positive attitude in life. Bad shots don't bother him much, and he knows they happen to everyone. "Golf is not about the quality of your good shots. It is about the quality of your bad shots."

When he was competing, he didn't want to overload his mind with golf, golf, golf. And that made him avoid a lot of socializing with other golfers as "I didn't want to talk golf all night," he said.

When putting, Nick points out it's very important to focus on keeping your wrists straight and you must have your hands moving in the direction you want to ball to travel. "Too many golfers focus on the ball and adjusting the putter head to line it up in the direction you want to go," said Nick.

It's important to be positive on the golf course. Nick said, "A year ago, I looked at a golf course and it was like 18 bear traps. I thought, 'How can I avoid getting my ankles bitten off?'"

"Now I am thinking good thoughts and planning my way around the course. And, I'm thinking, 'Let's make some birdies and see what score I can shoot.'"

You get positive by allowing yourself to understand bad shots happen and it is an opportunity to learn. "You have to give yourself the opportunity to mess up, or you are never going to learn from it."

"It's all about playing in the heat of the battle. You can do well in a major, but you can jostle through and avoid the real pressure. To be in there leading, going home Friday and Saturday with the lead, it's a different ball game. …Most past champions have all had seven to 10 years of paying their dues. It's like any major profession, like qualifying as a doctor." – Nick Faldo

KEEGAN BRADLEY

"I focus on my jaw muscles. When you can get your jaw to relax, this makes your whole body relax."

Keegan Bradley was born in 1986, is 6'3" tall and weighs 190 lbs. and was named Rookie of the year on Tour in 2011. His pre-shot routine and pre-putt routine are unique, as he fidgets a lot. His fidgeting is usually something golf coaches tell you not to do. But whatever works – works. Keegan has already won almost $20,000,000 during his PGA Career and continues to earn. He has already won over $1,000,000 on the PGA 2018 tour and currently ranks 24th on the money list as of the time of this writing.

Keegan's father, Mark Bradley was the head pro at the Jackson Hole Golf and Tennis Club and later moved to another golf club in New Hampshire. His father inspired Keegan.

Keegan decided in high school to make golf his profession.

Keegan starred at collegiate golf playing for St. John's University in NYC and won many collegiate tournaments.

In 2011, Keegan started on the PGA Tour. He didn't waste time winning a major. He won the PGA Championship beating Jason Dufner in a playoff. He was later named PGA Rookie of that year.

Keegan has a lot going on inside himself as he moves around more than other PGA Pros when playing a competitive round.

Keegan learned physical ways of getting himself relaxed, like relaxing his facial muscles before hitting a shot.

Most psychologists agree to force your body to do something like smiling, will make you feel happier. It's been proven that intentionally making physical movements with your face or body can help you have actual feelings of happiness and sadness, even if you aren't happy or sad.

In a well-known 1989 research project by renowned Psychology professor Robert Zajonc PhD., Dr. Zajonc had people make the "e" vowel sound and hold the "eee" sound.

When the human body makes the "eee" sound, your face automatically smiles happily.

Dr. Zajonc then made people make the "u" sound and hold the "uuu" sound. When the human body makes the "uuu" sound, your face automatically frowns or gives your face a sad look.

The people who made these sounds had no reason to feel happy or sad, but those making the "eee" sound reported feeling happy, and those making the "uuu" sound reported feeling sad.

So, Keegan has a good point in making your facial muscles relaxed. When the human body does this, you feel relaxed.

Keegan's pre-shot routine varies. "Keegan always has something new in his routine every time I play with him," said Jason Dufner, who himself also has a unique pre-shot routine.

By the way, Jason Dufner is known for his waggling the club before he hits a shot. Jason explained his waggling, "I played a lot of baseball growing up, and I always hit better if I kept moving before the pitch instead of standing still in the batter's box."

"I think a waggle does the same thing in the golf swing. It keeps you relaxed and gets your body ready to hit the ball."

Keegan's pre-shot routine goes like this: He stands behind the ball, taking 10-12 or more practice swings. He twirls his club by flipping the blade 360 degrees several times, fixes his hat, steps in, steps back, stares down at the ball, etc., etc.

Keegan said, "I catch a lot of dissension for it on tour from Dufner and these guys - they make fun of me ... and I have to take it."

Pre-shot routines are of course, unique to each golfer. Keegan said, "There's not a person in the world that does what I do."

Keegan added when you begin your swing, "You can't swing with hesitation."

Keegan gets focused and even though the kidding goes on about his unusual and long pre-shot routine, he's a good example of whatever you find works for you, do it.

Try relaxing your facial muscles the next time you're on the tee, or when you must make a putt. It does relax you and you'll play better golf.

People at times may tell you to relax after you shanked a tee shot. Have you ever told yourself to relax? Most find just telling yourself to relax won't do it.

So, Keegan gives an example of doing something to cause you to relax and reduce stress.

Here is an exercise you can try to see if this works for you. Pretend something bad just happened such as a mishit, OB, slow play, etc. which makes you tighten up and feel tense. Relax your face and mouth and count to 10 until you feel you're relaxed.

Or, if anything extremely annoys you and you feel tense, take your stance as if you're about to strike the ball or about to putt, feel the tension, then relax your facial muscles in the same manner and count to 10. Keep repeating this until it becomes second nature to help you relax.

Researchers have found that forcing your muscles to do something like relaxing or smiling does reduce stress. For more on this see, "Grin and Bear It: The Influence of Manipulated Positive Facial Expression on the Stress Response," which is published in the Journal Psychological Science. https://www.psychologicalscience.org/

"When I throw a softball, there's no time to think about the motion of my arm. I just look at the first baseman's glove and react.

"Most amateurs are so worried about mis-hitting the shot or hitting it offline, they don't make an aggressive move. You'd be surprised how much better your swing will get if you let your natural athletic ability shine. So go after it."

- Keegan Bradley

SERGIO GARCIA

"When I make practice swings on the tee I'm practicing for balance and tempo."

Sergio was born in 1980, stands 5' 10" tall, and weighs 180 lbs.

His father, Victor Garcia, a Spanish club pro, taught Sergio how to play golf from the time Sergio was three years old.

He did very well as an amateur and turned professional at 19. Sergio was ranked in the top 10 PGA Tour players for most of his career.

Sergio believes the tempo of your swing is a key factor in scoring well. He doesn't want to rush his swing. Having the right tempo, or speed of your swing is what gets you in the zone.

"When you make a few practice swings on the tee, think 'Tempo' first. Notice that I never make them at full speed. I'll make a nice, controlled move back and through. I'm not practicing for power. I'm practicing for balance."

It's tough for recreational golfers to get into a zone on a crowded Saturday golf round when you're experiencing delays, tee backups, and catching up with your fellow players, etc.

When Sergio won the Master, he said, "I've looked at the course differently the whole week."

"It's not a golf course I'm most comfortable in, because I fade the ball more than I draw the ball and you have to draw the ball at Augusta."

"But I knew that I could still work it around...I just accepted what was happening. So, I'm very proud of that."

Sergio won the Masters on Seve Ballesteros' 60th birthday if Seve hadn't died of cancer before his time.

Sergio said Olazabal (a former Masters Champion) contacted him before the tournament. "He told me what I needed to do - believe in myself. Be calm and not let things get to me."

Sergio won his first major at Augusta. He was relaxed, didn't force anything, and let the shots just happen.

Sergio had been known to take a lot of time with his pre-shot routine, fidgeting too much with gripping and re-gripping his club before hitting the ball, but he doesn't do that anymore. His main concern is the tempo of his swing.

He stands behind the ball taking practice swings. Then he selects his target and visualizes the shot. He aligns the shot and picks a spot (blade of grass or mark) 3 or 4 feet in front of his ball to line up the shot.

He addresses the ball and takes his stance. He looks at this target once more, takes a few waggles, and settles his feet comfortably.

He pauses briefly, then hits the ball.

Sergio does core and strength exercises in the gym. His website, sergiogarcia.com, shows what he does to work out in the gym at the time of this writing.

Sergio's recent marriage to Angela Akins, a former college golfer for the University of Texas and reporter for the Golf Channel (they've been dating since 2015), seems to have made Sergio stronger and more confident.

At the Masters, Sergio played very well being under pressure from Justin Rose, who he beat on the first playoff hole. Sergio did all this playing in a relaxed way.

"When I'm playing my best - it's when I don't think about my swing. I trust my setup and make a smooth swing."

- Sergio Garcia

PHIL MICKLESON

"When I'm going for the pin, I stay aggressive, and I get more into the shot."

Phil is the oldest player ever to win a major championship when he won the 2021 PGA Championship at Kiawah Island on the Ocean Course. He accomplished this great historical event by winning his 6th major in May 2021 cheered on by enthusiastic fans.

During his acceptance speech, he gave a big thank you to his coach, Andrew Getson, an Australian who Phil acknowledged as the person who "straightened out his swing." Andrew moved to the US in 2009 to play on the Nationwide Tour that is now known as the Korn Ferry Tour and then took up coaching full time in Scottsdale, Arizona. Andrew has also coached Kevin Streelman, who did exceptionally well at the 2021 PGA Championship and placed in the top 10.

Phil was born in 1970, stands 6'3" tall, and weighs 200 lbs. When he was 3 years old, he began playing golf. He would run off by himself to the golf course not telling his parents. His mother said, "Sometimes, he told neighbors he was going to the golf course while he was on his way there."

David Feherty said, "Phil's mother told me, 'Phil was so clumsy as a little boy, we had to put a football helmet on him until he was 4 because he kept bumping into things.'"

"I told her, 'Mary, Mary, I'm a writer, you can't keep handing me material like this.'"

"So, the next time I saw Phil I said, 'You didn't really wear a football helmet in the house until you were 4, did you?'"

"He said, 'It was more like 5.'"

Phil's father was an airline pilot, and his mother worked a second job to help support her son on his Junior Golf career.

Phil values winning and setting a good example. Phil won many tournaments in his teens (three times an American Junior Golf award winner), and because of his success in Junior Golf, he received a full scholarship to Arizona State. He graduated and had a remarkable NCAA career.

Phil said he's very aggressive and maintains he plays his best golf that way as he gets more focused and a better result in his shots. "

He then turned pro after college when he was 21 years old and became one of the most successful golfers of all time.

His pre-shot routine is multi-faceted. He considers many factors in each shot. He first establishes how far he can hit a club under the existing conditions. Let's say he normally hits his 8-iron 160 yards.

Phil knows that the 8 iron to go 160 yards changes depending on the wind, the temperature, the altitude of the course, the fact that golf balls travel farther in warmer temperatures - there is a difference playing the colder morning rounds than warmer afternoon rounds.

If he's playing in the morning, there may be dew and water on the ball which Phil knows increases spin and the ball travels less than a dry ball.

He considers the lie of the ball. If he's hitting an approach shot to the green, he needs to know the grain of the green and the various slopes on the green. He then determines how he wants the ball to come into the green.

He processes these factors, as well as any other relevant factors, and decides on a club and how he is going to hit the shot. Phil said, taking all the factors into account is important. "That's why I've been known to be such an accurate iron player."

Phil didn't play in the 2017 U.S. Open, and instead did something more important to him – he wanted to be at his daughter's high school graduation, and she gave the valedictorian speech.

Phil takes in many factors when putting as well. Phil's best putting tip is to make sure your putter head is properly aligned with the path you want the ball to take. "You can have the most beautiful putting stroke, but the stroke itself is minor, consistent setup, reading greens and aiming the putting face is more important."

In the final round at the 2021 PGA Championship, Phil took his time, walked casually, and played the round as golf announcer described as "Smart with a capital S."

"A great shot is when you pull it off. A smart shot is when you don't have the guts to try it."

- Phil Mickelson

ARNOLD PALMER

"Amateurs should putt from off the green if you can cleanly hit the ball, since their worst putt is usually better than their best chip."

Arnold Palmer was born in 1929 and passed away in 2016. He stood 5' 10" tall and weighed 185 lbs. An inspiration to golfers everywhere, and one who brought golf into the limelight, Arnie would be followed by thousands of fans, "Arnie's Army", when he played golf tournaments.

He won 92 Professional golf tournaments, including 7 major golf tournaments, and won the Masters 4 times.

He was inspired to play golf by his father, Deacon "Deke" Palmer, who was the resident pro at the Latrobe Country Club.

His father was tough on Arnie. "He taught me playing golf is not an easy road, and he was right. It hasn't been easy."

"He didn't throw accolades my way for all the great things I was doing."

Arnie explained, "He didn't want to puff me up too full of myself."

"My father told me, 'You don't need to tell anybody how good you are. You show them how good you are.'"

Arnie said, "So, I learned early not to brag about how good I was."

Arnie had humble beginnings. "I grew up on the wrong side of the tracks near a golf course and I saw how people lived on the other side of the tracks, who were the wealthy people at the golf club."

Arnie explained, "We had chickens and pigs in our yards. And we butchered every year. I'll never forget those things."

Arnie said, "We didn't have so much analysis and drills for every inch of the swing as we do today. I learned the game the simple way, practice fundamentals and the rest will follow."

Arnie had a simple pre-shot routine where he would first align the clubface behind the ball along the path he wanted it to start on.

Next, he'd plant his feet and set his feet in a comfortable position making sure the ball was properly placed in his stance to get the trajectory he wanted the ball to fly on.

Then he'd check to see if his feet and shoulders were lined up with the target.

In his pre-shot routine, Arnie had a well-known waggle which kept him loose and eased the tension.

Before each shot, he would waggle the club over the ball several times before hitting it.

During the waggles, he would be adjusting his grip making small corrections to his grip until it felt right. Then he'd hit the ball.

Arnie wouldn't give up when competing. "I've always made a total effort, even if my chances seemed very slim, I never quit trying"

When Arnie makes a putt, he kept perfectly still and held his breath. His only moving parts were his arms and hands.

If he overshot the hole by three feet, he wasn't shy on the second putt. "Many golfers have to fight off tensing up when they hit their second putt after putting it too far past the hole," Arnie said. "You know the line, so hit the second putt firm and smooth - without hesitation."

Arnie said to always try, if possible, to leave your second putt as an uphill putt. He pointed out that "An uphill putt has the back of the cup as a backstop. A downhill putt is just the opposite and has less chance of going in the hole."

Arnie used an old-fashioned barber pole (with red, white, and blue stripes turning in a spiral) as a reminder to turn on an axis when swinging. He'd keep his legs slightly bent and would twist his upper body without swaying making good contact with the ball.

If he found himself swinging too fast and missing his target, Arnie said, "My best cure for swinging too fast is I try to concentrate on getting the club back deliberately away from the ball bringing he club back slowly for the first few inches."

"If I want to make good contact, I keep my head still, plant my feet firmly, keep my balance, and get comfortable."

Arnie recommends taking the club away "in one piece, without breaking your wrists" for at least a foot when driving the golf ball. "This will get your upper body turning," Arnie said.

Arnie also believed an amateur golfer should putt rather than chip when you can cleanly hit the ball from off the green to the pin. "Your worst putt should always be better than your best chip in this situation."

Arnie said, "If you don't believe me, try putting 10 balls from off the green, then chip 10 balls from the same spot off the green, and you'll see what I mean."

For chipping, Arnie recommended you brush the grass with the clubhead like you were sweeping the ball off the grass on its way toward the pin.

On sand shots, Arnie would keep his legs quiet with knees bent. He'd, swing with his arms only which kept him from swaying or moving up or down on the shot. "Using just arms made my sand shots more consistent and made it easier for the leading edge of the clubhead to enter the sand in the exact spot I wanted it to."

Arnie knew the golf grip is very important. He'd take his time putting his left hand on the club, holding it in his fingers and diagonally crossing the palm of his left hand.

He would check to see two knuckles on his left hand with the crease between his thumb and forefinger facing his right shoulder. Then he quickly added his right hand once his left hand was in the proper position.

He was a multifaceted man and described golf as requiring complete concentration and total relaxation."

"Arnold Palmer? It was amazing how people reacted to him."

"He took energy from that and turned right around and gave it back."

– Tim Finchem, PGA Tour Commissioner

JON RAHM

"If I don't believe in myself, nobody is going to do it for me."

Jon Rahm was born in 1994, in a small town in Spain and said, "My father wanted me to play golf in America." He played golf for Arizona State University and stands 6'2" and weighs 220 lbs.

He's a star on the PGA Tour even though most thought he would play the European tour. Well-known Spanish golfers inspired Jon, "I wanted to play golf since I was a child because of the example set by Seve Ballesteros and Jose Maria Olazabal."

At Arizona State, Tim Mickleson (Phil's brother) coached Jon, and he played a lot of golf with Phil.

"Phil told me even before I turned pro, I would be one of the top 10 best players in the world."

Jon added, "I was like, 'okay, he's just trying to be nice, right? It's not possible.'"

"But, you know, once I turned pro, I started believing he was right and I'm pretty close to getting to that point." Jon is ranked #2 in the world in 2018 at the time of this writing.

Jon won 11 collegiate tournaments, second only to Phil Mickleson who had 16. He turned pro after being low amateur at the US Open.

Jon Rahm is an excellent example of what confidence and golf skill can do for a young player's attitude when starting out playing golf at the highest level.

When Jon played the Tournament Players Championship in Ponte Vedra Beach, he said, "A year ago I was in college watching this event. It's gone well for me so far. I'm not a perfectionist, but I expect a lot of myself. If I don't believe in myself, nobody is going to do it for me."

He doesn't get down on himself and has a good confidence level in his game. When he won the Farmers Insurance Open, he said, "First-timers usually don't have a great history at Torrey Pines…. I won that, and I keep it in mind. There's nothing that says I'm going to play bad, or I should play bad."

But sometimes the confidence level gets low, especially with a bad lie. Adam Hays is Jon's caddie, and they had a dramatic event at the 2019 Players Championship at the TPC at Sawgrass.

Jon said, "Adam was trying to convince me to go right, and when I first got to the ball I was really sure I could hit the green. I mean, if you give me 10 balls besides that one I'll hit all of them on land. But unfortunately, I got a little bit of doubt in me."

Jon hit it in the water and lost the tournament. And that, Jon said, can be done easily when you lose your momentum.

"If you can just somehow keep the momentum going and battle out those tough times you might be able to keep a round going. If you completely derail, which can happen really easily, you lose your swing, you lose your touch, it's hard to get it back."

BOBBY JONES

"You must be at ease, comfortable and relaxed at the address position."

Bobby Jones was born in 1902 and was 5'8" tall and weighed 165 lbs. He played as an amateur, and his excellent play created a lot of interest and enthusiasm for the game of golf.

He was 5 years old when his father, a lawyer, moved the family next to the East Lake Golf Course in Atlanta. Bobby had some health issues and the doctor told him to take up golf which he excelled at as a boy winning almost every tournament at East Lake.

Bobby was coached and taught the game by the Club Pro at East Lake, Stewart Maiden, who came to the US from Carnoustie, Scotland.

Bobby won the "Grand Slam," by winning all four major golf tournaments of his era and played 31 major golf tournaments in the US and UK and won 13 of those tournaments while placing in the top 10 almost 90% of the time.

Bobby retired from Golf at the age of 28 voluntarily ending a very short and extremely successful career.

He practiced law and continued to write about golf and helped found and design The Augusta National Golf Club.

He wrote "Golf is My Game," a book published in 1960, which described his style of play, and his ideas on how to play successful golf, and describing the fundamentals and the golf swing.

"My conception of the correct golf swing is built entirely around the one thought of assuring a full backward turn or wind-up of the trunk during the backswing."

He stressed being comfortable and relaxed during the golf swing. "You must be at ease, comfortable and relaxed at the address position."

His description of the swing was very simple, "The trunk must be turned around the spine as an axis under a motionless head, I think the player must truly 'move freely beneath himself.'"

In 1960, the concept of a pre-shot routine wasn't as common as it is today.

Bobby wrote, "A golfer needs to standardize the approach to every shot, beginning even before taking the address position."

Bobby felt the need for standardization of the approach since, "The more I fiddled around arranging the position, the more I was beset by doubts which produced tension and strain."

He described his pre-shot routine very simple. There were 4 steps.

1) "I began to approach every shot from behind the ball looking towards the hole."

2) "I would stop a little short of what my final position would be, just near enough to the ball to reach it comfortably."

3) "From there, the club was grounded, and I took one look towards the objective."

4) A waggle. "One waggle was begun while the right foot moved back to its place. When the club returned to the ground behind the ball, there was a little forward twist of the hips, and the backswing began."

Bobby didn't like more than one waggle. "Whenever I hesitated or took a second waggle, I could look for trouble."

The "forward twist of his hips was necessary, and he described why he did this in detail.

"The little twist of the hips I have mentioned is a valuable aid in starting the swing smoothly, because it assists in breaking up any tension which may have crept in."

"The movement is in the legs, and its chief function is to assure a smooth start of the swing by setting the hip turn in motion. Without it, the inclination is strong to pick the club up with the hands and arms without bringing the trunk into use."

Jack Nicklaus did the same but used a slight turn of his chin to his left before he took the club away on the upswing. Jack said he did this to remind himself to do a smooth takeaway and not pick the club up away from the ball.

Bobby stressed the point about being relaxed and comfortable to make a good golf shot.

"It is important to make the movement easy, smooth, and comfortable and to form the habit of getting the thing done without too much fussing and worrying."

BROOKS KOEPKA

"You have to stop yourself from thinking ahead. You can't start thinking about the trophy or about other things."

Brooks Koepka was born in 1990, stands 6 feet tall and weighs 186 lbs. and has done very well on the PGA Tour. He played golf on his high school team where he excelled and later played for the Florida State University team.

His father, Bob Koepka, a scratch golfer, taught both of his sons, Brooks, and Chase, how to play golf.

After finishing college, he turned professional and began playing The Challenge Tour in Europe and later the European Tour. Brooks qualified for the 2013 U.S. Open but missed the cut. He later qualified and finished tied for 12th in the Scottish Open.

Brooks played in the 2014 U.S. Open and finished fourth earning his PGA Tour Card.

Brooks explained later he put a lot of pressure on himself to get his card. "I only had seven spots to really get my card over here, so every shot and everything else was super important for me."

He won the 2017 U.S. Open and ranked 11th in the 2017 World Golf Rankings. He finished 16 under par winning the U.S Open, tying Rory McIlroy's record for the lowest U.S. Open finishing score.

He and Dustin Johnson are good friends. Dustin called him the night before the start of the final round of the U.S. Open and said, "One shot at a time. Stay patient and just keep doing what you're doing and try not to get ahead of yourself."

After Brooks won, he realized the more patient he becomes, the more times he will be in contention to win tournaments.

Brooks gained a lot of confidence by winning the U.S. Open. "Any time you can win, it's special, and if you're going back to those places, it's cool, you are kind of reliving some of the shots you hit, and obviously you get a lot of positive memories." This thought is something an average golfer can keep in mind when he goes back to play a course he scored very well on before.

Brooks now looks at competitive golf this way. "I don't really think too far ahead and that stops me from getting nervous."

He said, "I thought thinking ahead would make me stray from my game plan." And he added, "If you stray from your plan, that's when the trouble starts."

He told himself before starting the fourth round of the US Open, "You're here to play golf. Just stick with it for the next 18 holes, have confidence and I will celebrate later."

Brooks' pre-shot routine begins with his visualization of the shot, then he takes his grip, aligns the shot, and takes his stance. He does a few waggles and makes sure he's well balanced with his feet in a comfortable position and implants his feet firmly into the ground.

He takes away the club with his arms in one piece and makes a full-body turn and coils with his left shoulder turning under his chin and begins his downswing with his back turned toward the target.

When putting, he takes a relaxed grip on the putter with his right thumb on the grip and his index finger pointing toward the ground. He tied for fourth on PGA average putting statistics with Rickie Fowler.

He stays physically fit and works out at the gym weightlifting regularly and works his core muscles extensively.

Brooks is coached by a Team of Coaches and has used Claude Harmon III and appears to be using Pete Cowen has been coaching Brooks and has won 4 major titles so far.

He always tries to maintain a good attitude and when you are doing well there are always people who want to knock you off the hill. "You're always going to have fans, and you're always going to have people that hate you. The people around me, they know who I am, and that's really all I care about." And he added, "Sometimes your haters are your biggest motivators."

When Brooks was asked why he plays well in Major tournaments, he explained his view. "You figure, at least 80 of them, I'm just gonna beat. From there, you figure about half of them won't play well, so you're down to about maybe 35. And then from 35, some of them, just pressure is just going to get to them. That only leaves you with a few more, and you just must beat those guys. One of the things I've learned the past couple of years is you don't need to win it. You don't need to try and go win it. Just hang around. If you hang around, good things are going to happen."

He explained further, "That's what has caused me an issue in the regular PGA Tour events. I've gone out on Saturday and tried to build a cushion. Maybe pressed a little bit too hard and gotten ahead of myself, where in the majors, I just stay in the moment. I never think one hole ahead. I'm not thinking about tomorrow, I'm not thinking about the next shot. I'm just thinking about what I've got to do right then and there. I kind of dummy it down and make it very simple, and I think that's what helps me."

"I just think that big events, you see the same guys, and we see Brooksy up there again. Guys who understand how to play tough golf courses and tough venues tend to be up there, whether there's crowds or no crowds."

    - Tiger Woods

GREG NORMAN

"You have to be aggressive at this game."

Greg Norman was born in 1955, and stands 6 feet tall, and weighs 180 lbs. Greg was ranked the World's #1 golfer for 331 weeks (that works out to 6.4 years of total time). The only other player who exceeded that was Tiger Woods.

Greg didn't strive to be World #1. "My goal was always to be the best I could be. Being the best you can be is infinite. There's always room to grow. There's always something new to learn. And there's always something new to do."

Greg would set goals for himself and he said, "You have to set goals at the right level for yourself – not too high, but high enough to make you work hard, and there is a realistic chance of attaining that goal."

Greg learned to play golf when he was 15 years old and was taught by his mother, Toini Norman, who had a single-digit handicap. Greg turned professional when he was 21 years old.

Greg went from a high handicap of 27 to scratch in only 18 months. Greg was inspired by Jack Nicklaus and read his book, "Golf My Way," which greatly impressed him.

His overall strategy in the shot-making was to, "Play the shot you've got the best chance of playing well."

But that doesn't mean to play conservatively. Greg loved to compete and played aggressively.

Greg felt the average golfer doesn't need to play conservatively either. "Aggressive play is even more important to the average player."

Greg said average players should, "Attack this game in a bold, confident, and determined way, and you'll make a giant leap toward realizing your full potential as a player."

Greg said not to blame it on bad luck - ever. "You create your own luck by the way you play. Bad luck doesn't really exist."

When you play badly, Greg said, "You start thinking too much. That's when you confuse yourself and hit bad shots."

How do you stop overthinking? Greg says to practice deep breathing, envision the shot, and stop second-guessing yourself. "The moment you second guess yourself, is the moment you let yourself down."

And don't ever say no matter what you do, you can't improve. "Don't get into anger or self-pity."

And don't think it's your fate to be a bad golfer since that brings you down further. "Fate has nothing to do with success or failure, because that is a negative philosophy that lowers one's confidence, and I'll have no part of it."

Shot making: "As I walk between shots, I let my mind wander to all sorts of non-golf things - to my kids, to my next fishing trip, or whatever - but when I'm playing my best, my mind clicks back into focus well before I reach the ball."

"At a point about 40 yards short of the ball I begin to analyze the situation that's facing me. I look at the tops of the trees to check the wind, I look at the pitch and roll of the green area to get an initial feel for the way the ball will roll, and I look at the people around the green to get depth perception. By the time I get to my ball, I'm fully focused on the shot."

"Some of my colleagues on Tour delay this type of thinking until they arrive at the ball. I'm not saying they're wrong, but I do recommend my method to all amateurs, and for one big reason - it will speed up play!"

Greg has been very aggressive and very successful in golf and the business world. "You get out of it what you put in. If you are timid in this world, you're not going to get much out of it."

And don't be concerned whether you win or lose. "It's not the victories that count to me. It's the quality of how you deliver your losses and the quality of how you deliver your victories."

Have you ever lost the "feel" of putts? You putt well on the first hole, then you lose your feel on the second hole unexplainably?

To avoid losing feel, Greg uses a putting technique which he refers to as "Hold the hold." Many golfers take a practice putting stroke and a relaxed grip and make the practice stroke exactly as they need to make a smooth putt. They then loosen their grip and regrip the putter (too tightly), when they attempt their actual putt.

Greg recommends if you make a nice practice putt, don't loosen your grip and "hold the hold" when you make the actual putt. Tom Watson and others used this "hold the hold" method very successfully.

Greg suffered back injuries which made it difficult for him to play The Champions Tour. Greg turned 50 in February 2005 but kept his distance from the senior golf circuit due to business demands and his back problems.

Greg felt he would have avoided the back injuries had golf fitness been more widely used during his golf career. Greg now spends an hour and a half to two hours daily in his gym.

Greg has gone on to have an illustrious business career just trying to be as good as he can be.

"I always wanted to be the best I could be at whatever I did. I didn't want to be the number one golfer in the world. I just wanted to be as good as I could be. I work hard, I push myself hard, and I probably even expect too much of myself."

Tried and True Advice

Over years of golfing, certain advice is well known. Most PGA professionals feel this advice is beneficial to almost every golfer. See what you think.

1) Most golfers, especially recreational golfers don't have the time or can afford advice from renowned golf coaches like Butch Harmon, Pete Cowan, or Phil Mickleson's coach, Andrew Getson. When playing golf socially, it usually is the person who has the highest handicap who offers the most unsolicited advice. It is always best to take a lesson with a PGA professional who can see your swing and properly advise you.

2.) Practice every day. It is better to practice 15 minutes a day than to skip a week or two without practicing.

3.) Practice tempo and timing. Distance comes from having the right timing resulting in longer distance.

4.) Practice the short game. That's where you score and improve the quickest.

5.) Practice putting from 10 feet or less. Most recreational golfers have most trouble with short putts. Making putts from 10 feet in will greatly improve your scores.

6.) Try not to get down on yourself and try to have fun and relax. It is hard to beat a perfect day on the course, and it's a time to laugh with your friends and enjoy a good relaxing time together. Your mental game and golfing ability will improve.

7. As Payne Stewart said, "But in the end, it's still just a game of golf, and if at the end of the day you can't shake hands with your opponents, and still be friends, you missed the point."

Happy Golfing!

Creating Your Pre-Shot Routine and a Good Attitude

"Attitude will always win over ability… A golfer has to learn to enjoy the process of striving to improve. That process, not the end result, enriches life." – Dr. Bob Rotella, an excerpt from Golf is Not a Game of Perfect

Pre-shot routines are very important for the mental game of golf. Psychological research has been done on pre-shot routines and it was found that "Professional golfers felt that a pre-shot routine kept their minds occupied so irrelevant thoughts did not interfere with their performance." [1]

8 Professional golfers (4 of which played the PGA Tour, one was from the Senior Tour, and three from other tours) were tested on the psychological benefits of the pre-shot routine. It was found from

---

[1] Journal of Excellence, http://www.zoneofexcellence.ca/Journal/Issue14/The_Experience_of_Preshot_Routines_among_Professional_Golfers.pdf

studying the professional golfers in this investigation that,

- A putting pre-shot routine should be made with a lot of detail to get bad things out of your mind and promote good focus.

- The pre-shot routine made all of them feel comfortable.

- The pre-shot routine helped them "see the shot."

- The routine helped shot consistency.

- It helped to control their emotions.

If you have a pre-shot routine already, and it works for you. Fine. Don't do anything.

If you feel it needs repair, or if you want to experiment with a new one, or if you make up a new one for yourself considering what some of the best do. Here is more information on pre-shot routines.

The fine players in this book all seem to agree a good pre-shot routine will help you block out the negative that tends to creep into your brain before you hit your shot, especially, an intimidating shot on a difficult course.

Many golfers don't have a pre-shot routine, or used to have one, or may use a short-abbreviated routine of what they did for years.

Keeping pace with the foursome in front of you may stop recreational players from doing a pre-shot routine.

A common way to speed up play is to get out of your golf cart while your rider is preparing to hit his shot and walk over to your ball. Once you get to your ball, start thinking and preparing and visualize your shot, where it will land, the club you will use, the swing you will use, etc., etc.

Then when it's your turn to hit, you can go right into your pre-shot routine and hit a much better shot. Avoid jumping out of your cart and quickly hitting the ball in the general direction you want to go.

Another way to speed up play is to have two pre-shot routines.

Develop one routine for intimidating golf shots where you need to make a good shot, such as trying to hit a water surrounded island or peninsula green where there is no room for error.

An example of a good pre-shot routine for an intimidating shot would be standing behind the ball and visualizing the golf shot including its flight, a draw, or a fade, where it will land, and how far it will roll. Imagine there is no water or other hazards – just you and the green.

Then make the proper alignment by selecting a small spot three feet in front of you on your target line.

Next, make 3 practice swings using the tempo you want to hit the ball with. Make the right grip for the shot. Go into your stance, check your ball position, grip, and get your feet comfortable, and set them.

Take one more look up at your target to briefly check alignment, then hit the shot.

A rough example of a short pre-shot routine would be three practice swings behind the ball, visualize the shot, take your stance, check ball position, set your feet comfortably, take one more look at the intended target, and hit the shot.

Many golfers have no idea when they address a ball where it is going to go other than wanting the ball to go into the general middle of the fairway or close to the pin on the green. Try picking a small landing area or envision the putt going into the hole.

Simple Ways to Keep a Good Attitude.

It is hard to beat a perfect day on the course, and it's a time to laugh with your friends and enjoy a good relaxing time together.

Here are some tips to help maintain a good positive attitude.

1. Before each shot and putt, have a clear picture in your mind of what you want to do. Keep that picture calmly as you do pre-shot routines and pre-putt routines. This will also help you to stay in the present with every shot.

2. View each shot or putt as a brand-new challenge. Appreciate each shot or putt as a new opportunity. If you hit a bad shot or putt, forget about it and view the next shot as a new challenge.

3. Bad shots happen. Don't let bad shots disappoint you. Instead, expect bad shots. Remember bad shots are learning opportunities. Don't let annoying "Coulda, woudda, shoudda" thoughts cloud your brain.

4. Don't give up. Even if your round is the worst in your life, your game can change with one good shot. Or think about trying to better the best score you ever made on the next golf hole. Think of making a good swing on your next shot.

5. Forget about your total score and instead treat each round as 6 rounds of 3 holes each.

6. Breathe slowly through your nose to slow your heart rate down and get more oxygen to your brain to help you keep calm.

7. Most everyone seems to love the huge, long drive straight down the middle. Love the short game even more. Love the chipping and love the putting and make your short game shine. Look forward to them with joy once you're around the green.

8. Don't just go to the practice range. Instead, find opportunities to practice on the course during off-hours to get familiar and practice on the most difficult areas of the course. Practice the difficult shots you dislike the most.

9. Smile. Walk straight and tall with confidence and pride. Hold your chest out at every opportunity. Acting confident breeds more confidence. Sam Snead said, "Could I have

whipped Tiger Woods? Hell, yes.... No man scared me on the golf course." Sam always stressed the importance of having confidence on the course. He suggested before a round or on your way to the course, reflect on all the good shots you've made in the past. Practicing will bring out your ability to do them again. Know this ability is already inside you.

Or you may even try forgetting about scoring well. Think of bad rounds as helping you to build character and be aware better rounds will happen in the future. Keep track on your scorecard when you lost control of your emotions and see if you can improve controlling your emotions each time you play with a goal of keeping calm for 18 holes.

That's it! But if you find yourself ruminating and extending your negative thoughts, you can stop it by challenging yourself to find new golf habits to keep the game fresh before you play. Consider exercising in private to get the blood flowing throughout your body, such as jumping jacks, toe touches, high-knees, burpees, etc. Or, simply stretching more while waiting to tee off.

"The greatest thing about tomorrow is, I will be better than I am today. And that's how I look at my life. I will be a better golfer, I will be a better

person, I will be a better father, I will be a better husband, I will be a better friend. That's the beauty of tomorrow."

— *Tiger Woods*

Afterword

Each PGA Tour player is unique, yet they seem to have the same philosophy of enjoying the game and playing the best they can by following what works.

The best players seem to be true to themselves and accept themselves yet at the same time, constantly try to improve.

When they find something that makes them play well, they follow it. If it stops working, they search and find something else that does work and so on and continue along that "process" in their professional career.

It is our wish that you (whether you are trying to get a PGA Tour card or just want to be a better player at your club or just want to play better socially) find that "process" that the best players constantly seek as an exciting and enjoyable journey in your life!

And, more importantly, we hope you find golf as an overall relaxing time to enjoy and share a drink with your friends.

What do you think? We'd be interested in hearing from you or feel free to post on our Facebook Group "Golf Jokes and Stories" with 157k members and growing. Or email us at

Bruce@teamgolfwell.com as we love to hear from our fans! Happy golfing!

As Dr. Bob Rotella advises, just doing the process of improving your game builds character and is an amazing journey that will benefit you all your life!

Happy golfing!

Thank You

Thank you for reading this book and we hope it will make golf more enjoyable for you.

If all else fails when playing, sometimes a good laugh solves it all, so you might want to check out our ever-growing 160k member Facebook Group, **"Golf Jokes and Stories."** Our amazing members constantly surprise us with posting new jokes and expressions of unique and brilliant wit about the game we love.

Above all, have fun playing golf and enjoy all your adventures and social golf contacts!

If you liked our book, and if you have the time, please give it a review on Amazon.

Thank you again and best to you!

The Ways of Golf's Greatests

About the Authors

TeamGolfwell are authors of over 35 books several of which are Amazon bestsellers in Golf Coaching and other categories.

More about the Team at Golfwell

Made in the USA
Las Vegas, NV
27 June 2025